English Connect

365+

English Connect

365+

Phrases

Eric Thompson

PARTRIDGE

A Penguin Random House Company

To order additional copies of this book, contact
Toll Free 800 101 2657 (Singapore)
Toll Free 1 800 81 7340 (Malaysia)
orders.singapore@partridgepublishing.com

www.partridgepublishing.com/singapore

INTRODUCTION

I want to congratulate you for having this book in your possession. I believe it will serve the purpose for which you have it and help you to connect.

Let me start by asking you this question:

Why do you speak? Or why do you want to speak at all?

The answer is simply to communicate or better still to connect with people.

We communicate by a) Asking questions **(WH & YES or NO** questions, also referred to as **Open/Closed ended questions).**

WH or open ended questions are also referred to as information questions, because you will give or get more information with them.

b) (i) Responding to questions(ii) Making statements.

These are done by mouth, body parts gesture or by writing. All may be used separately or altogether at the same time.

A question may be:

1. A Request.
2. Asking for permission.
3. An Offer to help or give something.
4. An Invitation.
5. Asking for information.
6. Seeking advice. etc.

You need to know how to ask questions in conversations, not only to answer questions. So, you will need to know the purpose or the reason why you want to ask a question so also is to know why someone asked you a question in a conversation.

Communication may start with a simple Smalltalk which may be either a question or a simple statement which may *connect* you to your destiny. Who knows?

> Smalltalk is made of predetermined set of phrases or ones that you can **cook up** yourself depending on the situation you may find yourself, used for starting a conversation with an acquaintance or even a total stranger.

So, let's work together through this simple but great resource that contains multi-words or phrasal verbs, prepositional phrases, chunks and useful expressions used mostly by native speakers daily.

Take advantage of the simplicity, make or **cook** your own sentences at the end of each phrase or expression, visualize and digest the tips in the Treasure boxes, don't just memorize, make them yours and see how easy it is to connect. Happy learning!

1. GET / SET THE BALL ROLLING

Meaning:

To start or to begin something or series of activities.

Example:

If I could just get the ball rolling, I know other people would help.

Now make your sentences.

1. _____.
2. _____.
3. _____.

2. I'M GETTING GOOSE BUMPS!!!

Example of conversation:

Harumi: This movie is so scary. I'm frightened to death!

Leo: Harumi, this isn't scary! This movie is for little kids!

Harumi: No it's not... oh, no! That monster is horrible! **I'm getting** goose bumps!

Leo: That "monster" is just a cute little elf! What's the matter with you?

Harumi: I've never been good with scary movies. They really freak me out.

Leo: You should try to relax. It's not real, it's just a movie!

Harumi: But how can you be so sure? Maybe this is a documentary and you don't even know it

Leo: No more of such nonsense! How can this be a documentary?

Meaning:

Goosebumps are small, raised lumps that appear on the skin because of cold, fear or excitement

Now make your sentences.

1. _____.
2. _____.
3. _____.

3. I HAVE SOMETHING...........

Meaning:
When using this expression, you are trying to communicate that you possess something or need to do something that may be vital.

Examples:
"I have something to share with you."
"I have something important to tell you."
"I have something to apologize about."

Now make your sentences.

1. _____.
2. _____.
3. _____.

4. I'D RATHER..........

Meaning:
This means you would like to do or prefer one thing more than another.

Examples:
"I'd rather talk about this later."
"I'd like to eat at home than go get fast food."
"I'd rather ski than snowboard."

Now make your sentences.

1. _____.
2. _____.
3. _____.

5. I FEEL LIKE ....

Meaning:
Here you are expressing to someone something you would enjoy to do.

Examples:
"I feel like going for a bike ride."
"I feel like going to the beach."
"I feel like having a snack."

By adding 'don't' or 'do not' you can change what you are saying to express something you would not enjoy or express a concern about something.

Example: I don't feel like going to the beach.

Now make your sentences in both situations.
1. _____.
2. _____.
3. _____.

6. I'm TRYING TO.....

Meaning:
'I am trying' informs someone that you are attempting to accomplish something using bodily or mental strength.

Examples:
"I'm trying to get a job."
"I'm trying to eat healthy."
"I'm trying to understand your explanation."

Now make your sentences.
1. _____.
2. _____.
3. _____.

7. GET ABOUT/AROUND

Meanings:
1) Move from place to place
2) Spread or circulate

Examples:

1) It is not easy to get around the city without a map.

2) News of their separation soon got about.

Now make your sentences.

1. _____.
2. _____.
3. _____.

8. FIT IN (WITH)

Meaning:

Feel comfortable or be in harmony with.

Example:

He just doesn't fit in with the others.

Now make your sentences.

1. _____.
2. _____.
3. _____.

9. EMBARK ON/UPON

Meaning:

Start or engage in something.

Example:

She embarked on a career that leads her to fame.

Now make your sentences.

1. _____.
2. _____.
3. _____.

10. EASE OFF/UP

Meaning:
Reduce, become less severe or slow down(pain, traffic, work etc).

Example:
After Christmas, the workload generally eases off.

Now make your sentences.
1. _____.
2. _____.
3. _____.

11. DIG INTO.

Meanings:
1) Try to find something deeply.
2) Start to do something.
3) Take from something.

Examples:
1) He dug into his pocket and found a coin.
2) She thought it was time to dig into the work that had accumulated on her desk.
3) Dad had to dig into his savings to repair the roof.

Now make your sentences.
1. _____.
2. _____.
3. _____.

12. COME FORWARD

Meaning: To present oneself.

Example:
The police have asked any witnesses to **come forward**.

Now make your sentences.

1. _____.
2. _____.
3. _____.

13. CHIP IN

Meaning:
Contribute to, or participate in, something done by a group.

Example:
Bob has decided to retire and we're going to buy him a present. Do you want to chip in?

Now make your sentences.

1. _____.
2. _____.
3. _____.

14. CATCH UP WITH

Meaning;
Reach the same stage as someone else.

Example:
I've missed some classes so I'll have to work hard to **catch up with** the others.

Now make your sentences.

1. _____.
2. _____.
3. _____.

15. CARRY OUT.

Meaning:
1) Do something as specified (plan, order).
2) Perform or conduct (test, experiment...).

Examples:
1) The plan was carried out to perfection.
2) Tests are carried out to determine the efficiency of a new drug.

Now make your own sentences.
1. _____.
2. _____.
3. _____.

TREASURE BOX 1: LEARN PHRASES.

> It's not only the vocabularies that you know, you need a lot of phrases/ phrasal verbs, idioms, chunks of words here and there too to be able to communicate and connect in a conversation.

16. BARGAIN FOR.

Example: The interview was more difficult than he had bargained for.
Meaning; Expected situation or situation prepared for.

Now make your sentences.
1. _____.
2. _____.
3. _____.

17. Bail Out.

Meanings:
1) Pay money to secure someone's release
2) Rescues from financial difficulties.

Examples:
1) When he was arrested, his family refused to bail him out.
2) The government bailed out the bank.

Now make your sentences.

1. _____.
2. _____.
3. _____.

18. "Lay Out"

Meaning: To lay out means to explain an idea or a plan clearly and in detail

Example:
The manager had spent a few days working out a plan to revive the company, and then he laid his ideas out at the meeting.

Now make your sentences.

1. _____.
2. _____.
3. _____.

19. "My feet are killing me"

Marie: You look a bit tired. What have you been doing?
Tomoko: Shopping for some new outfits.
Marie: Did you get what you want?
Tomoko: I did, but it took me all day.
Marie: What do you want to do now?
Tomoko: I just want to sit down somewhere and relax. My feet are killing me!

Meaning:

If you say that something is killing you, you mean that it is causing you physical or emotional pain.

Now make your sentences.

1. _____.
2. _____.
3. _____.

20. "LIKE THERE IS NO TOMORROW"

Libby: What's in that bag? Whatever it is, I bet it was expensive.
Penny: It's a new cocktail dress, absolutely irresistible.
Libby: That's the second dress you've bought this month and you've already bought three pairs of new shoes.
Penny: A girl needs to look her best at all times.
Libby: But you've been spending like there's no tomorrow.
Penny: Do you want me to go round looking like a tramp?

Meaning:

If someone does something like there is no tomorrow, they do it very fast, in large amounts and without thinking carefully

Now make your own sentences.

1. _____.
2. _____.
3. _____.

REVIEW: 1

Choose a phrasal verb to replace the explanation in brackets.

1. Every morning I (stop sleeping) _____ _____when I hear the alarm clock.

   a) wake out   b) wake up   c) wake in   d) wake off

2. On Sundays I can (leave bed) _____ _____ later.

   a) get out   b) step off   c) get up   d) step out

3. We must (be quick) _____ _____ or we'll be late for school!

   a) act up   b) fasten on   c) hurry up   d) speed in

4. John helped the old lady to (board) _____ _____ the bus.

   a) mount on   b) get on   c) get up   d) put on

5. Julie went to the library to (try to find) _____ _____ a book.

   a) look out   b) look after   c) look for   d) look up

6. It's time for the news. Let's (start) _____ _____ the radio.

   a) turn on   b) tune in   c) turn up   d) tune at

7. "Please come in and (have a seat) _____ _____" said the doctor.

    a) seat up   b) seat down   c) sit up   d) sit down

8. When Dad arrives home, he (removes) _____ _____ his coat.

    a) puts off   b) takes off   c) leaves in   d) takes out

9. Dad couldn't see very well. "(wear) _____ _____ your glasses" said Mum.

    a) put on   b) put away   c) put in   d) put up

10. When we arrive at the station, we (descend from) _____ _____ the train.

    a) get down   b) stand down   c) get off   d) stand out

21. STEP UP

Meaning:
Filling in for someone or doing well at an important thing.

Example:
When his father was sick with the flu, the 12 year old son
stepped up and helped his mother do all the stuff his dad usually does. The whole family was proud.

Now make your sentences.
1. _____.
2. _____.
3. _____.

22. STEP DOWN

Meaning:
To gently quit a high level job without quitting or being fired.

Example:
On his 85th birthday, his father stepped down and let his son run the family business.

Now make your sentences.
1. _____.
2. _____.
3. _____.

23. BUY OFF.

Meaning:
Buy off means to give money to (someone) for illegal or dishonest help.

Example:
Many believe that the criminal *bought off* the police so that he would not be investigated for the murder.

Now make your sentences.
1. _____.
2. _____.
3. _____.

24. CROP UP.

Meaning:
Crop up means, to come or appear when not expected.

Examples;
   1. New problems *crop up* every day.
   2. His name *crops up* frequently as a potential candidate.

Now make your own sentences.

1. _____.
2. _____.
3. _____.

25. WEED OUT.

Meanings and examples:

To *weed out* is to remove (people or things that are not wanted) from a group

1. They will review the applications to *weed out* the less qualified candidates
2. He *weeded out* several unsuitable models before he found the right car.

Now make your sentences.

1. _____.
2. _____.
3. _____.

REVIEW: 1. ANSWER

Choose a phrasal verb to replace the explanation in brackets.

1. Every morning I (stop sleeping) __wake___up__when I hear the alarm clock

   a) wake out   **b) wake up**   c) wake in   d) wake off

2. On Sundays I can (leave bed) ____get up__ later.

   a) get out   b) step off   **c) get up**   d) step out

3. We must (be quick) ___hurry up _____ or we'll be late for school!

   a) act up   b) fasten on   c) hurry up   d) speed in

4. John helped the old lady to (board) __ get on__ the bus.

   a) mount on   **b) get on**   c) get up   4) put on

5. Julie went to the library to (try to find) __look for__ a book.

   a) look out   b) look after   **c) look for**   d) look up

6. It's time for the news. Let's (start) ___turn on _____ the radio.

   a) turn on   b) tune in   c) turn up   d) tune at

7. "Please come in and (have a seat) _____sit down _____" said the doctor.

    a) seat up   b) seat down   c) sit up   **d) sit down**

8. When Dad arrives home, he (removes) __takes off _____ his coat.

    a) puts off   **b) takes off**   c) leaves in   d) takes out

9. Dad couldn't see very well. "(wear) __put on _____ your glasses" said Mum.

    a) put on   b) put away   c) put in   d) put up

10. When we arrive at the station, we (descend from) _____get off __ the train.

    a) get down   b) stand down   **c) get off**   d) stand out

26. EMPTY OUT..

Meaning: To remove everything from inside something

Example:
1. The cops stopped the boys and told them to empty out their pockets.
2. I knew I'd been promoted when the boss smiled and told me to empty my old desk out and take everything to the office next to his.

Now make your sentences.
1. _____.
2. _____.
3. _____.

27. BE AFTER.

Meaning: To want to have or get something of someone.

Examples:

1. Don't believe a word he says. He is only after your money.
2. I am after an unusual present for my husband, do you have any ideas?
   Check your dictionary for more after combinations(look after, take after etc.)

Now make your sentences.

1. _____.
2. _____.
3. _____.

28. GET A GRIP.

Example.

A. I've got exams, I haven't worked, I don't feel well. It's all going wrong!

B. Get a grip! The exams are next month, so you've got plenty of time to revise.

Meaning:

We use this phrase to tell someone to stop worrying about something and to control themselves.

Now make your sentences.

1. _____.
2. _____.
3. _____.

29. RUN AROUND.

Example

A. How was your meal last night?

B. The food was great, but I think one of the staff was off sick because they were all ***running around like headless chickens***.

Meaning

This phrase is used to describe a panic group of people.

Now make your sentences.

1. _____.
2. _____.
3. _____.

30. IT'S MY TREAT.

Katsuya: You look tired. Would you like to have a cup of coffee with me? It's my treat.
Nancy: OK. Caffeine is exactly what I need right now.
Katsuya: How is everything going?
Nancy: As usual, I keep visiting clients, working on proposals and making phone calls.

Explanation:
Treat - Payment of something for another person.

Now make your sentences.

1. _____.
2. _____.
3. _____.

TREASURE BOX 2: HERE IS A LIST OF COMMON SMALL TALK SUBJECTS.

Sports, Hobbies, Weather, Family, Media, Holidays,
Home town, Job, Latest fashion and trends, Celebrities etc.
Remember; always ask general questions not too specific ones.

31. ACHE FOR...

Meaning:
To want something or someone very much.

Example:

*He was so lonely he **ached for** the sound of a human voice.*

Now make your sentences.

1. _____.
2. _____.
3. _____.

32. ANSWER FOR...

Meaning:
1) To be responsible for something.
   or
2) To speak on behalf of someone.

Examples:

*1) Normally parents have to **answer for** their children's behavior.*

*2) I agree, but I can't **answer for** my associate.*

Now make your sentences.

1. _____.
2. _____.
3. _____.

33. APPEAL TO.

Meaning:
1) To plead or make an earnest request.
2) To be attractive or interesting.

Example:

*1) The organizers **appealed to** the crowd to stay calm.*

*2) Camping doesn't **appeal to** me.*

Now make your sentences.

1. _____.
2. _____.
3. _____.

34. ADVISE AGAINST.

Meaning:

To recommend not doing something.

Example:
*The doctor **advised** him **against** carrying heavy loads.*

Now make your sentences.

1. _____.
2. _____.
3. _____.

35. BELIEVE IT OR NOT.

Meaning:

This phrase is used to tell someone something unusual but true.

Example:

A. What did you do at the weekend?
B. Well, believe it or not, my boyfriend took me to New York as a surprise!
C. Wow! Lucky you!

Now make your sentences.

1. _____.
2. _____.
3. _____.

36. I JUST DON'T GET IT.

Meaning;
This phrase is used to express that we cannot understand the reason for something.

Example;
A. Bill should be here by now. It's eight o'clock. We're going to miss the start of the movie.
B. I just don't get it. He told me he really wanted to see it.

Now make your sentences.

1. _____.
2. _____.
3. _____.

37. HAVE A SECOND THOUGHT.

Stanley: Are they interested in working with us?
Raymond: Not for now. They said that they would love to accept our deal if the price was negotiable.
Stanley: I see. What's your opinion?
Raymond: They don't have enough budget, I don't like to work with people who bargains over prices.
Stanley: Raymond, I think you're a good salesman but you haven't show any passion with your job recently. You give up easily; I believe if you show enough aggressiveness to your clients, they would have a second thought.
Raymond: OK. I will **pay them** a visit tomorrow.

Meaning:
To have second thoughts means, to change your opinion about something.

Now make your sentences.

1. _____.
2. _____.
3. _____.

38. WHY THE LONG FACE?

Meaning:
If you have a long face, you look sad.

Example:
A. 'Why've you got such a long face?'
B. 'My boyfriend doesn't want to see me anymore"

Now make your sentences.
1. _____.
2. _____.
3. _____.

39. ON THE SAME PAGE

Meaning:
To be thinking in a similar way

Example:
My boss said she called the meeting to make sure everybody's on the same page.

Now make your sentences.
1. _____.
2. _____.
3. _____.

40. COME A LONG WAY

Meaning:
To make a lot of progress and improvement.

Example:
Computer graphics have come a long way in the last few years.

Now make your sentences.

1. _____.
2. _____.
3. _____.

REVIEW: 2

Choose a phrasal verb to complete the following sentences.

1. The meeting had to be_____ _____(to a later date) because of the strike.

    a) set off   b) put off   c) laid off   d) set to

2. The films begins at 8.30. I'll _____ you _____ at 8.15.

    a) pick/up   b) take/out   c) collect/up   d) run/up

3. Tom is depressed. He's finding it difficult to _____ _____ his divorce.

    a) get over   b) get past   c) go after   d) give away

4. There is no more sugar. Never mind, we can _____ _____ it!

    a) dispense of   b) make up   c) take off   d) do without

5. Teaching is not easy. Sometimes teachers have to _____ ____ aggressive children.

    a) handle to   b) deal with   c) cope on   d) work out

6. Alan met Julie by accident. He _____ _____ her at the supermarket.

    a) walked into   b) crashed into   c) bumped into   d) banged into

7. The boss wants an explanation. How do you ___ _____ the decrease in sales?

   a) make up   b) break down   c) add up   d) account for

8. If we _____ _____ of petrol on this isolated road, we'll be in trouble!

   a) lack in   b) run out   c) stay out   d) roll out

9. Sometimes fighting _____ _____ among supporters at soccer matches.

   a) takes off   b) starts up   c) breaks out   d) rises up

10. There will be no press conference tomorrow. It has been _____ _____.

   a) called off   b) taken back   c) put away   d) set off.

41. BEAR FRUIT.

Meaning:
To **bear fruit** is to produce a desired result or reward.

Example: All his plans have finally **borne fruit**.

Now make your sentences.
1. _____.
2. _____.
3. _____.

42. SKIM THROUGH SOMETHING

Meaning:
To read through something hastily.

Example:

She skimmed through the catalogs, looking for a nice gift for her husband.

Now make your sentences.

1. _____.
2. _____.
3. _____.

43. SKIN SOMEONE ALIVE

Meaning:

To be very angry with someone; to scold someone severely.

Example:

If Idon't get home on time, my parents will skin me alive.

Now make your sentences.

1. _____.
2. _____.
3. _____.

44. VOUCH FOR

Meaning:

To pledge that something will be performed in a specified manner.

Example:

I cannot vouch for the accuracy of the story.

Now make your sentences.

1. _____.
2. _____.
3. _____.

45. AS I SEE IT / IN MY OPINION / IN MY VIEW.

Meaning:
The way I think about it

Example:
This whole affair has been overblown, as I see it.

Now make your sentences.

1. _____.
2. _____.
3. _____.

TREASURE BOX 3: HERE IS A LIST OF TOPICS THAT AREN'T VERY GOOD FOR SMALL TALK.

Salary, Politics, Relationships, Religion, Death, Financial, and Sales especially to someone you have just met.

46. EVEN OUT

Meanings;
1) Remove differences of opinion.
2) Become level or regular

Example;
1) After a long discussion they managed to even out their differences.
2) The road was evened out to make it safer.

Now make your sentences.

1. _____.
2. _____.
3. _____.

47. BRANCH OUT.

Meaning:
To begin to do more different kinds of activities or work

Example:
The company specializes in casual clothing but it is branching out into formal wear.

Now make your sentences.
1. _____.
2. _____.
3. _____.

48. GET ABOUT/AROUND

Meanings:
1) Move from place to place
2) Spread or circulate

Examples:
1) It's not easy to get around the city without a map.
2) News of their separation soon got about.

Now make your sentences.
1. _____.
2. _____.
3. _____.

49. YOU'VE GOT TO BE KIDDING

Meaning:
This expresses a surprise at something that you think cannot be true.

Example:

A: "Hey Kate. Mom told me to tell you that you shouldn't stay out too late."

B: **"You've got to be kidding me.** I'm 28 years old."

Now make your sentences.

1. _____.
2. _____.
3. _____.

49. LIVE THROUGH

Meaning:

To experience something and survive

Example:

My grandparents lived through two wars.

Now make your sentences.

1. _____.
2. _____.
3. _____.

50. HANG OUT

Meaning:

To spend time in a particular place or with a group of friends

Examples:

1. Where do you hang out these days?
2. Who do you hang out with?

Now make your sentences.

1. _____.
2. _____.
3. _____.

REVIEW: 2. ANSWER

Choose a phrasal verb to complete the following sentences.

1. The meeting had to be _ b__ (to a later date) because of the strike.

   a) set off   **b) put off**   c) laid off   d) set to

2. The movies begins at 8.30. I'll _____ you _____ at 8.15.

   a) pick/up   b) take/out   c) collect/up   d) run/up

3. Tom is depressed. He's finding it difficult to _____ _____ his divorce.

   a) get over   b) get past   c) go after   d) give away

4. There is no more sugar. Never mind - we can to _____d_____ it!

   a) dispense of   b) make up   c) take off   **d) do without**

5. Teaching is not easy. Sometimes teachers have to _____ ____ aggressive children.

   a) handle to   **b) deal with**   c) cope on   d) work out

6. Alan met Julie by accident. He _____c_____ her at the supermarket.

   a) walked into   b) crashed into   **c) bumped into**   d) banged into

7. The boss wants an explanation. How do you ____ d____ the decrease in sales?

   a) make up   b) break down   c) add up   **d) account for**

8. If we ____b____ of petrol on this isolated road, we'll be in trouble!

   a) lack in   **b) run out**   c) stay out   d) roll out

9. Sometimes fighting __ c____ among supporters at football matches.

   a) takes off   b) starts up   **c) breaks out**   d) rises up

10. There will be no press conference tomorrow. It has been ____a _____.

    a) **called off**   b) taken back   c) put away   d) set off.

51. IRON OUT

Meaning:
To resolve or eliminate differences, quarrels or misunderstandings by discussion.

Example:
The meeting tomorrow will be an opportunity to iron out difficulties.

Now make your sentences.

1. _____.
2. _____.
3. _____.

52. GIVE A GO.

Meaning:
We use this expression to say we will try something or to encourage someone else to try something for the first time, even if it is unusual.

Example:
Kane: Have you ever played underwater hockey?
Jake: No, but I'd be happy **to give it a go.** It sounds like fun.

Now make your sentences.
1. _____.
2. _____.
3. _____.

53. MISS OUT (ON).

Meaning.
This phrase means to lose an opportunity to do something.

Example:
If you leave before Saturday you'll miss out on the party.

Now make your sentences.
1. _____.
2. _____.
3. _____.

54. NAME AFTER

Meaning:
To give the same name as another person.

Example:
William was named after his grandfather.

Now make your sentences.

1. _____.
2. _____.
3. _____.

55. WATCH THE PAINT DRY

Example:
"I have a good salary, but my job is as boring as watching paint dry."

Meaning:
If something is extremely boring, you can say that it is like watching paint dry.

Now make your sentences.

1. _____.
2. _____.
3. _____.

56. IT OCCURRED TO ME THAT......

Meaning:
You use this phrase to let someone know your thought about something or that you suddenly remembered or found out.

Examples:
1. It occurred to me later that I forgot your birthday."
2. "It occurred to me that we both belong to the same gym."
3. "It occurred to me that eating healthy makes me feel better."

Now make your sentences.

1. _____.
2. _____.
3. _____.

57. LIGHT UP

Meaning:
To Illuminate.

Examples:
1) 1 watched the floodlights light up the castle.
2) Her face always lights up when she sees her grandson.
3) The screen lights up when you turn on a computer.

Now make your sentences.
1. _____.
2. _____.
3. _____.

58. PLAY DOWN

Meaning:
Minimize or make something appear less important

Example:
The government played down the gravity of the situation.

Now make your sentences.
1. _____.
2. _____.
3. _____.

59. PLAY UP

Meaning:
Emphasize or exaggerate or make something seem more important.

Example:
He always plays up his achievements.

Now make your sentences.

1. _____.
2. _____.
3. _____.

60. POP UP

Meaning:

Arise, occur

Example:

The question *popped up* during the meeting.

Now make your sentences.

1. _____.
2. _____.
3. _____.

REVIEW: 3

Complete the following sentences with the best options.

1. They hope to ____ _____ a contract and sign it before the end of the week.

   a) set up   b) put up   c) draw up   d) make up

2. He's a very dependable person. You can ____ __ him in any circumstances.

   a) count for   b) trust in   c) stand for   d) rely on

3. Many husbands avoid any housework. They manage to ____ _____ ___ it.

   a) get safe of   b) go past on   c) stay away of   d) get out of

4. I'm glad you're coming to the meeting. I _____ _____ to meeting you.

   a) look ahead   b) look forward   c) see forward   d) think ahead

5. Harry reads the newspaper every morning. He likes to _____ _____ _____ the latest events.

   a) stand up to   b) stay on to   c) keep up with   d) get up to

6. Tom and Bill had a meeting in order to _____ _____ their difficulties.

   a) bash out   b) wash out   c) iron out   d) spread out

7. Tests will be _____ _____ to determine the causes of the failure.

    a) taken up   b) carried out   c) looked into   d) run on

8. The plans for the new theater _____ _____ _____ a lot of criticism.

    a) ran up to   b) faced up with   c) came up against d) was opposed to

9. Sophie wants to leave the company. We'll have to _____ _____ a way to make her stay.

    a) set up   b) turn out   c) figure out   d) stumble on

10. Anyone can make a mistake but George never _____ _____ to his errors.

    a) comes on   b) owns up   c) goes forward d) pays up

61. SCALE BACK/DOWN

Meaning:
Make something smaller than originally intended.

Example:
Due to the crisis, the company had to scale down the size of the plant.

Now make your sentences.
1. _____.
2. _____.
3. _____.

62. SETTLE FOR...

Meaning:
To accept something that is not quite satisfactory.

Example:

I was hoping for a better proposal but I'll settle for the amount you offer.

Now make your sentences.

1. _____.
2. _____.
3. _____.

63. SIGN OVER TO

Meaning:

Transfer ownership of something

Example:

He signed over the house to his two children.

Now make your sentences.

1. _____.
2. _____.
3. _____.

64. SHOP AROUND

Meaning:

When you shop around you compare prices.

Example:

It's always wise to shop around before buying anything.

Now make your sentences.

1. _____.
2. _____.
3. _____.

65. SINGLE OUT

Meaning;
This phrase means, to be selected for special attention.

Example;
Two boys were singled out for extra coaching.

Now make your sentences.

1. _____.
2. _____.
3. _____.

TREASURE BOX:4

Phrasal verbs are part of a large group of verbs called "multi-word verbs" which are important part of the English language. They are very common, especially in spoken English. Study them and make them yours.

66. TAKE AWAY

Take away 1.
Meaning:
To buy food at a restaurant and carry it elsewhere to eat it.

Example:
Two beef curries to take away please.

take away 2.
Meaning
Cause something to disappear

Example;
The doctor gave me tablets to take away the pain.

Now make your sentences.

1. _____ .
2. _____ .
3. _____ .

67. TAKE BACK

Meaning: 1
Agree to receive back/ be returned.

Example;
We will take back goods only if you can produce the receipt.

Meaning: 2
Retract or withdraw something that was said

Example;
I take back what I said about cheating.

Now make your sentences.

1. _____ .
2. _____ .
3. _____ .

68. TAKE IN

Meanings and examples;

1. Allow to stay in one's home
   She's always taking in stray cats and dogs!
2. Note with your eyes and register.
   She **took in** every detail of her rival's outfit.
3. Understand what one sees, hears or reads.
   The man immediately took in the scene and called the police.

Now make your sentences.

1. _____.
2. _____.
3. _____.

69. TAKEOUT.

Meanings and examples;

1. To remove or extract something
   She took out a pen to note the address.
2. To invite someone to dinner, the theater, cinema, etc.
   He took her out for a meal on her birthday.

Now make your sentences.

1. _____.
2. _____.
3. _____.

70. TALK ...OUT OF.

Meaning;

Persuade someone not to do something.

Example;

I tried to talk Grace out of leaving her job.

Now make your sentences.

1. _____.
2. _____.
3. _____.

1. They hope to ____d_____ a contract and sign it before the end of the week.

    a) set up   b) put up   c) draw up   d) make up

2. He's a very dependable person. You can ____d__ him in any circumstances.

    a) count for   b) trust in   c) stand for   d) rely on

3. Many husbands avoid any housework. They manage to _ d_ it.

    a) get safe of   b) go past on   c) stay away of   d) get out of

4. I'm glad you're coming to the meeting. I ____ b___ to meeting you.

    a) look ahead   b) look forward   c) see forward   d) think ahead

5. Harry reads the newspaper every morning. He likes to _____c_____ _____the latest events.

    a) stand up to   b) stay on to   c) keep up with   d) get up to

6. Tom and Bill had a meeting in order to _____c_____ their difficulties.

    a) bash out   b) wash out   c) iron out   d) spread out

7. Tests will be ____b_____ to determine the causes of the failure.

    a) taken up   b) carried out   c) looked into   d) run on

8. The plans for the new theater _____c_____ a lot of criticism.

   a) ran up to b) faced up with c) came up against d) was opposed to

9. Sophie wants to leave the company. We'll have to _____c_____ a way to make her stay.

   a) set up   b) turn out   c) figure out   d) stumble on

10. Anyone can make a mistake but George never _____b_____ to his errors.

   a) comes on   b) owns up   c) goes forward   d) pays up

71. THINK OVER

Meaning;
To consider the result of doing something, before making a final decision.

Example;
I'll have to think over the proposal before I decide.

Now make your sentences.
1. _____.
2. _____.
3. _____.

72. HOLD BACK".

Meanings and Examples
1. To stop yourself from showing something.
   Susan couldn't hold back her tears when she heard the news that her grandmother had died.
2. To prevent something from progressing.
   The lack of funding held the project back.

Now make your sentences.

1. _____.
2. _____.
3. _____.

73. SEND BACK

Meaning;

To return something, especially by mail.

Example;

My letter was sent back to me because I used a wrong address.

Now make your sentences.

1. _____.
2. _____.
3. _____.

74. SET UP

Meanings and Examples

1. To arrange or organize
   Our boss set a meeting up with the president of the company.
2. To trick or trap
   The police set up the car thief by using a hidden camera.

Now make your sentences.

1. _____.
2. _____.
3. _____.

75. STICK TO

Meaning;

To continue doing something or to limit oneself to one particular thing.

Example;

You will lose weight if you stick to the diet.

Now make your sentences.

1. _____.
2. _____.
3. _____.

TREASURE BOX:5

Be patient with yourself when it seems you are not progressing, push yourself, but do not beat yourself. Keep a right attitude and keep practicing.

76. GO OVERBOARD

Example:

"That woman looks like a clown! She definitely went overboard with her makeup!"

Meaning:

If you go overboard, it can mean that you fall off of a boat, but it usually means that you do too much of something.

Now make your sentences.

1. _____.
2. _____.
3. _____.

77. PAY OUT.

Meaning:

To pay a large sum of money to somebody.

Examples:

1. If you win the lottery, they'll **pay** the money **out** in installments over several years.
2. Most insurance companies will try to find any reason to avoid paying outclaims to their customers.

Now make your sentences.

1. _____.
2. _____.
3. _____.

78. DEVOTE TO.

Meaning:
To give a lot of your time or money to an activity or a person.

Example:

1. Rowland devotes more time to his family than to work.
2. She devoted her life to helping the poor.

Now make your sentences.

1. _____.
2. _____.
3. _____.

79. DIE DOWN

Meaning:
If something dies down, it gradually becomes weaker in strength or lower in volume or magnitude.

Example:
The new president waited for the applause to die down before he began to speak.

Now make your sentences.

1. _____.
2. _____.
3. _____.

80. COME ALONG

Meaning:
To go with somebody when they're going somewhere

Example:
1. We're going to the beach for a swim. Do you want to come along?
2. My brother really wants to see this movie, is it OK if he comes along as well?

Synonym: Tag along.

Now make your sentences.

1. _____.
2. _____.
3. _____.

REVIEW: 4

Complete the following sentences with appropriate prepositions
(after by at in from into away off on to about for with)

1. I asked my neighbor to look _____ my cat when I went to London.

2. All books are provided __ the school. Pupils don't have to pay _____
    them.

3. The meeting is _____ September 15th _____ 9 a.m.

4. If you're interested __ working overseas, you should apply _____ that
    job

5. London is a big city, but it's very different _____ New York.

6. My boss got angry _____ me when I arrived late _____ the second time.
    7. I'm not familiar__ this machine. Could you explain _____ me how it
    works?

8. She wrote the text _____ Japanese, then translated it _____ English.
    9. He left the house, got _____ his car and drove _____.

10. Due to bad weather conditions, the plane couldn't take _____ _____ time.

11. She was embarrassed _____ the way people were staring _____ her.

12. They apologized _____ the host _____ arriving late

13. The authorities talked _____ the need _____ better education in
    developing countries.

14. _____ my opinion, you should wait _____ confirmation before making
    a decision.

15. Students often have problem _____ English prepositions.

81. TAKE THE PLUNGE.

Meaning:
To make a decision to do something, especially after thinking about it for a long time

Example:
They're finally taking the plunge and getting married.

Now make your sentences.
1. _____.
2. _____.
3. _____.

82. BE OR FEEL FLATTERED.

Meaning:
To feel very pleased and proud because someone has said good things about you or has made you feel important

Example:
They were flattered to be invited to dinner by the mayor.

Now make your sentences.
1. _____.
2. _____.
3. _____.

83. A TIGHT SCHEDULE

Meaning:
A tight schedule means very busy.

Example:
I am on a tight schedule. Can you help me out with this project?

Now make your sentences.

1. _____.
2. _____.
3. _____.

84. I'M NOT SURE IF ....

Meaning:

'This phrase expresses a feeling of uncertainty or lack of confidence on a particular matter.

Examples:

"I am not sure if they will offer me the job."

"I'm not sure if she'll return my call."

"I'm not sure if I understand your question."

Now make your sentences.

1. _____.
2. _____.
3. _____.

85. BEAT ABOUT (AROUND) THE BUSH.

Meaning:

To avoid coming to a conclusion.

Examples:

1. Stop beating about the bush; tell me what you're here for.
2. There is no point in beating about the bush. I'm leaving.

Now make your sentences.

1. _____.
2. _____.
3. _____.

REVIEW: 4. ANSWER

Complete the following sentences with appropriate prepositions:
(after by at in from into away off on to about for with)

1. I asked my neighbor to look _____after_____ my cat when I went to London.

2. All books are provided _by_ the school. Pupils don't have to pay __for___ them.

3. The meeting is ____on__ September 15th __at____ 9 a.m.

4. If you're interested _in_ working overseas, you should apply __for_____ that job

5. London is a big city, but it's very different ____from /to_____New York.

6. My boss got angry __at_____ me when I arrived late __for____ the second time.

7. I'm not familiar_ with_ this machine. Could you explain __to__ me how it works?

8. She wrote the text ____in____ Japanese, then translated it ____to____ English.

9. He left the house, got ____in____ his car and drove ____off___ .

10. Due to bad weather conditions, the plane couldn't take _____off __on__ time.

11. She was embarrassed _____by__ the way people were staring ____at__ her.

12. They apologized ____to____ the host ___for____ arriving late

13. The authorities talked ____on___ the need ____for____ better education in developing countries.

14. ___In___ my opinion, you should wait __for____ confirmation before making a decision.

15. Students often have problem ____with___ English prepositions.

86. HARD TO SWALLOW.

Example:

"It was hard to swallow the news that everyone at our company was being fired."

Meaning:

If something is hard to swallow, it means it is hard to believe.
This phrase is similar to **a bitter pill to swallow.**

Now make your sentences.
1. _____.
2. _____.
3. _____.

87. YOUR GUESS IS AS GOOD AS MINE

Example:

"I don't know where we are, and neither do you, so your guess is as good as mine about which way we should go."

Meaning:

If you say your guess is as good as mine, you are telling someone that you don't know what the correct answer is.

Now make your sentences.
1. _____.
2. _____.
3. _____.

88. IN THE BLACK

Example:

"Our business has been in the black since we opened three years ago."

Meaning:

In the black is a phrase to describe that a company or business, is profitable, or making money.

The opposite is, in the red, which means a business is losing money.

Now make your sentences.

1. _____.
2. _____.
3. _____.

89. IF I WERE YOU, I WOULD ......

Here you are advising someone of what YOU would do in a given situation.

Examples:

"If I were you, I would enjoy my vacation."
"If I were you, I would answer his phone calls."

By adding 'have' after the word 'would' you are talking about the past.

Examples:

"If I were you, I would have enjoyed my vacation."
"If I were you, I would have answered his phone calls."

Now make your sentences.

1. _____.
2. _____.
3. _____.

90. UP IN ARMS.

Example:

"The town's residents were up in arms about the proposed tax increase."

Meaning:
If you are up in arms ("about something" or "over something"), then it means you are unhappy and are complaining about it.

Now make your sentences.

1. _____.
2. _____.
3. _____.

TREASURE BOX:6

> Remember that verbs determine sentences in so many ways. They will tell you whether you are talking about now-present or the past or the future.

91. BENT OUT OF SHAPE

Example:
"I know you're unhappy about your test score, but you shouldn't get bent out of shape over it.

Meaning:
This phrase means you feel really angry and upset about something.

Now make your sentences.

1. _____.
2. _____.
3. _____.

92. MESS UP.

Meaning and examples:

1: To mess up is to make a mistake or to do something incorrectly.

   * I messed up on my first attempt and had to try again.

2. To make (something) dirty or untidy.
   * Don't mess up my room.
3. To damage or ruin something.
   * She's really messed up her life.
   * His life has been messed up by his drug addiction.

Now make your sentences.
1. _____.
2. _____.
3. _____.

93. SPILL THE BEANS

Example:
"Your gift was supposed to be a surprise, so I'm sorry I **spilled the beans** and told you what it is."

Meaning:
If you **spill the beans**, it means you tell something that was supposed to be a secret, either because you made a mistake, or because you don't care that it was a secret.

Now make your sentences.
1. _____.
2. _____.
3. _____.

94. PULL THE PLUG

Example:
"We've spent a lot of money and wasted a lot of energy, but I think it's time to pull the plug on this project, because it seems it's never going to work properly."

Meaning:
If you pull the plug on something, it means you stop supporting it or you stop it from functioning.

Now make your sentences.
1. _____.
2. _____.
3. _____.

95. OVER THE TOP.

Meaning:
Over-the-top means, too extreme, unusual, excessive or extravagant.

Example:
I thought the decorations were way over the top.

Now make your sentences.
1. _____.
2. _____.
3. _____.

96. BREAK INTO.

Meanings and Examples:
1: To enter (a house, building, etc.) illegally and especially by using force.
    *Someone tried to break into our house while we were away.

2: To begin to do or have (something) suddenly.
    *She broke into tears. [=she suddenly began to cry]

3: To interrupt (something).
    * The network broke into the program with a special news report.
    * I couldn't help but break into their conversation.

Now make your sentences.

1. _____.
2. _____.
3. _____.

97. WRITE OFF

Meaning;
To give up on someone or something as a loss, waste of time, hopeless, useless, unimportant etc.

Example;
Don't write me off yet, I will do my best and surprise you.

Now make your sentences.

1. _____.
2. _____.
3. _____.

98. ABIDE BY.

Meaning;
To accept and obey a decision or a set rule or regulation.

Example;
Most drivers abide by the rules of the road.

Now make your sentences.

1. _____.
2. _____.
3. _____.

99. HEAD BACK

Meaning;
To start moving back to the original place.

Example;
I walked to the end of the street and then headed back home.

Now make your sentences.
1. _____.
2. _____.
3. _____.

100. WALK AND CHEW GUM

Example:
This is an easy job, and if you can walk and chew gum, then you should be able to do it.

Meaning:
If you can walk and chew gum, it means that you can do two things at the same time.

Now make your sentences.
1. _____.
2. _____.
3. _____.

REVIEW: 5

Choose a phrasal verb to replace the explanation in brackets.

1. When Caroline goes to work, the babysitter (takes care of) _____ _____ the children.

    a) looks at   b) looks up   c) looks for   d) looks after

2. The babysitter (has a good relationship) _____ _____ well with the children.

    a) gets out   b) gets on   c) gets up   d) gets in

3. Peter promises he will (stop) _____ _____ smoking soon.

    a) give in   b) give over   c) give up   d) give out

4. They (continue) _____ _____ talking when the teacher arrives.

    a) carry on   b) get on   c) break out   d) remain on

5. The fire fighters came and (extinguish) _____ _____ the fire.

    a) put off   b) let away   c) put out   d) let out

6. I'll call the shop to (discover) _____ _____ the price.

    a) find out   b) bring out   c) turn up   d) call up

7. You never forget the place where you (spend childhood) _____ ___

    a) bring up   b) raise up   c) grow up   d) rise up

8. If your car (ceases to function) _____ _____, you should call a garage.

    a) stops off   b) breaks down   c) turns off   d) breaks out

9. It's difficult for a plane to (leave the ground) _____ _____ when there is snow on the ground.

    a) take off   b) start up   c) lift off   d) rise up

10. You must (return) _____ _____ the books that I lend you.

    a) hand in   b) take back   c) give back   d) pay for

101. SHOOT FROM THE HIP.

Example:
It's best to think before you speak, and not shoot from the hip.

Meaning:
If a person shoots from the hip, that means they say or do something without thinking about it first.

Now make your sentences.
1. _____.
2. _____.
3. _____.

102. ROLL THE DICE

Example:
"Let's roll the dice and see what happens!"

Meaning:
If someone rolls the dice, that means they take a chance or do something risky.

Now make your sentences.

1. _____.
2. _____.
3. _____.

103. KICK THE CAN DOWN THE ROAD.

Meaning:
kicking the can down the road means delaying and hoping that a problem will disappear instead of solving the problem.

Example:
Instead of solving problems, the government just kicks the can down the road.

Now make your sentences.

1. _____.
2. _____.
3. _____.

104. PULL THE WOOL OVER ONE'S EYES.

Meaning:
To pull the wool over one's eyes is to deceive someone.

Example:
"Most politicians pull the wool over everyone's eyes, because they only care about being reelected."

Now make your sentences.

1. _____.
2. _____.
3. _____.

105. NO DICE

Meaning:

The phrase no dice is a way of saying "not possible".

Example:

I called the movie theater to see if they still had tickets, but they told me, 'no dice – the movie is sold out'.

Similarly, "**No soap**".

Example:

We were looking for a house to rent on the island but it was no soap.

Now make your sentences.

1. _____.
2. _____.
3. _____.

TREASURE BOX:7

How can you make yourself understood? Mimic native speakers. Watch your intonations, pronunciations and tonic syllables where you stress your verbs or phrasal verbs in conversation.

106. "THANKS BUT NO THANKS"

Example:

A. You could earn double by working in the city, you know?

B. ith all the pollution, the crime, the stress. *Thanks but no thanks*.

Meaning:

We use this expression to decline an offer someone has made, or to give a negative opinion of something we don't want to or wouldn't want to do.

Now make your sentences.

1. _____.
2. _____.
3. _____.

107. "GROW ON TREES".

Example:

Mike: Dad, can I have a new bike?"

Dad: We can't afford one now. Money doesn't **grow on trees** you know.'

Meaning:

This phrase means to exist in large amounts or to be easy to get.

Now make your sentences.

1. _____.
2. _____.
3. _____.

108. "TIED UP"

Example:

Cameron: Hey! Can we talk?

Anna: I'm kind of tied up at the moment.

Cameron: When can I call you back then, it's really important?

Anna: It's noon here. How about four hours from now?

Cameron: I'll be in bed then. I've got an eight o'clock meeting.

Anna: Call me before you go, then.

Cameron: Okay, talk to you later.

Explanation:
When someone is tied up, they are busy or are prevented from doing something, such as speaking to someone or going somewhere.

Now make your sentences.
1. _____.
2. _____.
3. _____.

109. "A MELTING POT"

Example:
Ramos: Does this just make you feel like you're back in Asia?
Yuki: It doesn't remind me of home, but it doesn't seem like Western Europe, either.
Ramos: Venice has always been a melting pot, a meeting place for East and West.
Yuki: I can see that with all this diverse architecture.
Ramos: Venice was like the Hong Kong of Europe. Traders passed through here for centuries.
Yuki: No wonder there are so many exotic things here!

Explanation:
Melting pot means a place where many different people and ideas exist together, often mixing and producing something new

Now make your sentences.
1. _____.
2. _____.
3. _____.

110. "LAY OUT"

Meaning:
To lay out means to explain an idea or a plan clearly and in detail

Example:

The manager had spent a few days working out a plan to revive the company, and then he laid his ideas out at the shareholders' meeting..

Now make your sentences.

1. _____.
2. _____.
3. _____.

Choose a **phrasal verb** to replace the explanation in brackets.

1. When Caroline goes to work, the babysitter (takes care of) ____d____ the children.

   a) looks at   b) looks up   c) looks for   d) looks after

2. The babysitter (has a good relationship) _____a_____ well with the children.

   a) gets out   b) gets on   c) gets up   d) gets in

3. Peter promises he will (stop) ____c_____ smoking soon.

   a) give in   b) give over   c) give up   d) give out

4. They (continue) _____a_____ talking when the teacher arrives.

   a) carry on   b) get on   c) break out   d) remain on

5. The fire fighters came and (extinguish) _____c_____ the fire.

   a) put off   b) let away   c) put out   d) let out

6. I'll call the shop to (discover) __a_____ the price.

   a) find out   b) bring out   c) turn up   d) call up

7. You never forget the place where you (spend childhood) __c__.

   a) bring up   b) raise up   c) grow up   d) rise up

8. If your car (ceases to function) __b____, you should call a garage.

   a) stops off   b) breaks down   c) turns off   d) breaks out

9. It's difficult for a plane to (leave the ground) ____a____ when there is snow
   on the ground.

   a) take off   b) start up   c) lift off   d) rise up

10. You must (return) ____c____ the books that I lend you.

    a) hand in   b) take back   c) give back   d) pay for

111. "NOT FEELING UP TO PAR"

Example:
Daniel: I was in the neighborhood and thought I'd stop by to see if you were
up for a drive.
Betty: No thanks. I'm not feeling up to par.
Daniel: Are you coming down with something?
Betty: No, my allergies are acting up.
Daniel: You still have them?
Betty: Yes, that's the story of my life. I've got the sniffles and a sinus headache,
and my eyes are itchy. Don't they look swollen?

Explanation:
To feel up to par is to feel well.
Not feeling up to par means not feeling well.

Now make your sentences.

1. _____.
2. _____.
3. _____.

112. "LET'S FACE IT"

Example:

A. Every day Jun tells me how much he loves Rolls Royce cars.
B. Yes, but let's face it, the only way he'll ever have one is if he steals it!

Meaning:
We use this expression to introduce a negative idea that we have to accept.

Now make your sentences.

1. _____.
2. _____.
3. _____.

113. "OUT OF CURIOSITY"

Example:

A. You weren't in when I called last night. ***Out of curiosity***, where were you?
B. Oh, yes. I was with some friends who I hadn't seen for years.

Meaning:
This expression means to do something because we are interested to know.

Now make your sentences.

1. _____.
2. _____.
3. _____.

114. "TURN OVER A NEW LEAF".

Meaning:
This idiom means to start behaving or living in a different and better way.

Example:
I decided to turn over a new leaf and stop worrying so much.

Now make your sentences.

1. _____.
2. _____.
3. _____.

115.

Alex: "You know, Amy, I must have been born under a lucky star. You're fine, the baby is fine, John and May are fine, and even Bingo is fine!"

Amy: "Oh that reminds me! Speaking of Bingo, he was sound asleep in his chair, and suddenly he sat bolt upright!"

Alex: "Wow, that's odd. Maybe he suddenly remembered a bone he had buried in the back yard!"

Amy: "I'm not sure what it was all about. He ran over to me and wanted me to pet him, so I did, and then he seemed content. Who knows?"

Meanings:
Born under a lucky star = very fortunate
Sound asleep = in a deep sleep
sit bolt upright = sit up very straight, usually suddenly

Now make your sentences.

1. _____.
2. _____.
3. _____.

116. "THERE ARE PLENTY OF FISH IN THE SEA"

Nick: What did you do when she said it was over?
Max: I went home.
Nick: Don't you love her?
Max: I like her but, there are plenty of fish in the sea.
Nick: Yes, but it's hard to catch any good ones.
Max: If they're all as jealous as Jessica, I'd rather throw them all back.

Explanation:
There are plenty of fish in the sea - means there are many other possibilities, especially when one thing has been unsuitable or unsuccessful.

Now make your sentences.
1. _____.
2. _____.
3. _____.

117. QUIT WHILE ONE IS AHEAD

Meaning:
To stop doing something after achieving success or atleast partial success.

Example:
My friend had won at slots, so he quit while he was ahead

Now make your sentences.
1. _____.
2. _____.
3. _____.

118. "ON A DAILY BASIS"

Example:
A. I love seafood, don't you?
B. Yes, but I wouldn't want to eat it ***on a daily basis.***

Meaning:
We use this phrase to talk about something that we do every day.

Now make your sentences.
1. _____.
2. _____.
3. _____.

119. "OVER THE MOON".

Gordon: Have you seen Johnny today?
Martin: No, why?
Gordon: Well he's clearly over the moon about something.
Martin: What about?
Gordon: He won't tell anybody, but I've never seen him looking so happy.
Martin: He's a betting man, so perhaps he's won a lot of money on the horses.

Explanation:
If you say that you are over the moon, you mean that you are very pleased or happy about something.

Now make your sentences.
1. _____.
2. _____.
3. _____.

120. WORKS LIKE A CHARM".

Salesman: Lowest prices! Best quality! Hello, sir!
Buyer: Oh, hi. I'm just looking. I have a computer already.
Salesman: How long have you had it?
Buyer: Years. Works like a charm.
Salesman: Years? What a dinosaur! I can't believe you still use it.
Buyer: It's fine for writing letters and...

Explanation:

If something works like a charm, it is very effective or successful.

Now make your sentences.

1. _____.
2. _____.
3. _____.

REVIEW: 6

Complete the following sentences with the right prepositions.
(after by at in from into away off on to about for with)

1. Mr. Martin is responsible _____ recruitment

2. I'm sorry but I don't understand the reason _____ the increase _____ price.

3. In this company, salaries depend _____ the level of responsibility.

4. You have to pay _____ the tickets the day you order them.

5. Our new Chairman reminds me _____ my old history teacher.

6. Do you think the report could be translated _____ English for the meeting tomorrow?

7. Thank you for offering to help. It's very kind _____ you.

8. Look _____ the woman _____ the picture. Who is she?

9. The manager didn't take part _____ the discussion. He didn't want to intervene.

10. It's no use taking him to the Louvre. He isn't interested _____ art.

11. The food in Japan is very different _____ European food.

12. I don't agree _____ you. _____ my opinion you're wrong.

13. John was late for the meeting as usual. That's typical _____ him.

14. We should invite Pete to the party. He's very good _____ telling jokes.

15. The car crashed _____ a fence _____ the other side of the road.

121. "SO FAR SO GOOD".

Example:
A. How's your new office assistant getting on?
B. *So far, so good.* He's settling in and there haven't been any big problems.

Meaning:
We use this expression to say that we are happy with the progress of a situation that has not yet finished.

Now make your sentences.
1. _____.
2. _____.
3. _____.

122. "CALL A SPADE A SPADE".

Meaning:
If you call a spade a spade, you tell the truth in a straightforward and direct way, even if the truth is not pleasant.

For example:
I should warn you that Sandra calls a spade a spade, so if she thinks you say or do something wrong, she'll say so.

Now make your sentences.
1. _____.
2. _____.
3. _____.

123. "TAKE YOUR MIND OFF SOMETHING".

Meaning:
This phrase means doing an activity to stop ourselves thinking about something unpleasant.

Example:

A. The exam's over now. There's nothing you can do about it now.

B. I know, but I'm still so worried I won't pass.

A. Why don't you go to the cinema and take your mind off it?

B. Thanks, that's a good idea

Now make your sentences.

1. _____.
2. _____.
3. _____.

124. SINK IN.

Meaning:

To *sink in* means to become completely known, felt, or understood.

Examples:

• I had to tell him what to do over and over before it finally *sank in*.

• The fact that she's left me still hasn't really *sunk in*.
   Look it up in your dictionary for more understanding.

Now make your sentences.

1. _____.
2. _____.
3. _____.

125. AT ARM'S LENGTH.

Meanings and Examples:

1. From a distance that is the length of a person's arm.
   *It's best to view the painting at arm's length.

2. To keep someone or something at arm's length is to avoid being very close to or friendly with someone or something.
   * Since going to college, he has kept his old friends at arm's length.

Now make your sentences.

1. _____.
2. _____.
3. _____.

TREASURE BOX:8

Prepositional phrases are set phrases that are introduced by prepositions. These set phrases are also often used with specific verbs. The placements of prepositional phrases are at the end or at the beginning of sentences.

126. ENVIRONMENTALLY CONSCIOUS.

Brett: Why are you saving those old plastic bags? Just throw them away.
Terri: No, I can't do that. I'm saving them to reuse them.
Brett: It's hardly worth the effort, surely.
Terri: Oh it is. One plastic bag reused is one less thrown away. And that's got to be good for the environment.
Brett: My, my, you are environmentally conscious.
Terri: And why not? We've all got a responsibility to protect the environment.

Explanation:
If someone is environmentally conscious, he is concerned about the impact that manufactured products eventually have on the environment.

Now make your sentences.

1. _____.
2. _____.
3. _____.

127. ON THE GO

Gloria: Freda! Put the kettle on. My feet are killing me and I'm dying for a cup of tea.
Freda: Had a hard day?

Gloria: I'll say. I've been on the go all day, hardly had a minute to sit down.

Freda: Why was that?

Gloria: Well, our store held a clearance sale today and our department was absolutely jam-packed with customers all day.

Freda: That's because nobody can resist a bargain.

Explanation: On the go means to be in constant activity or very busy.

Now make your sentences.

1. _____.
2. _____.
3. _____.

128. THE SAME OLD STORY

Example

A. Why is Barbara crying?

B. It's *the same old story*. She's had another argument with her boyfriend.

Meaning:

We use this expression to say that we are in a situation that has happened before. Normally this is a negative situation.

Now make your sentences.

1. _____.
2. _____.
3. _____.

129. "WHAT I'M TRYING TO SAY IS..."

Example:

A. Your work is not good, you're often late, and you don't seem to care.

B. I'm sorry - it won't happen again.

A. No. What I'm trying to say is that if you don't change, I'll have to fire you.

Meaning:

We use this expression to point out our actual meaning.

Now make your sentences.
1. _____.
2. _____.
3. _____.

130. NOTE DOWN

Meaning:

If you *note down* something, you write it on a piece of paper or in a notebook.

For example:

*note down something

Can I borrow your pen, please? I just need to *note down* this address in case I forget it.

*note something down;

Leon took a moment to *note the number down*.

Now make your sentences.
1. _____.
2. _____.
3. _____.

REVIEW: 6. ANSWER

Complete the following sentences with the right prepositions:
(**after by at in from into away off on to aboutfor with**)

1. Mr. Martin is responsible ____for____ recruitment.

2. I'm sorry but I don't understand the reason _____for_____ the increase ____in_____ price.

3. In this company, salaries depend _____on_____ the level of responsibility.

4. You have to pay _____for_____ the tickets the day you order them.

5. Our new Chairman reminds me ____of_____ my old history teacher.

6. Do you think the report could be translated _____into____ English for the meeting tomorrow?

7. Thank you for offering to help. It's very kind _____of___ you.

8. Look _____at_____ the woman ____in_____ the picture. Who is she?

9. The manager didn't take part _____in_____ the discussion. He didn't want to intervene.

10. It's no use taking him to the Louvre. He isn't interested _____in____ art.

11. The food in Japan is very different _____to_____ European food.

12. I don't agree _____with___ you. _____in_____ my opinion you're wrong.

13. John was late for the meeting as usual. That's typical _____of_____ him.

14. We should invite Pete to the party. He's very good _____at_____ telling jokes.

15. The car crashed _____into_____ a fence _____on___ the other side of the road.

131. It's better than nothing

Jim: Did you ask Mr. Davidson for a raise?
Carmen: Yes, I asked for 80 cents any hour more.
Jim: Did you get it?
Carmen: No, I got 30 cents
Jim: That's too bad.
Carmen: OH, it is alright. It is better than nothing.

Explanation:
This expression means you got less than you expected, but it is better to have that thing than to have nothing at all.

Now make your sentences.
1. _____.
2. _____.
3. _____.

132. Have a soft spot.

Example:
I **have a soft spot for** the people of Malaysia, because they were very nice to me when I lived there.

Definition:
If you **have a soft spot for** something or someone, it means that you have **fond**, or affectionate, feelings for it or them.

Now make your sentences.
1. _____.
2. _____.
3. _____.

133. SMELL A RAT.

Example:
Linda: I was almost fooled by a telephone call I had yesterday.
Becky: Not one of those telling you that you had won a wonderful prize.
Linda: Yes, a week's vacation for two. It sounded great.
Becky: What made you smell a rat?
Linda: When they told me I had to ring a special telephone number to claim the prize. Then I was sure it was a scam.
Becky: Yes, those calls are charged at unbelievably high rates.

Meaning:
If you smell a rat, you begin to suspect or realize that something is wrong in a particular situation.

Now make your sentences.
1. _____.
2. _____.
3. _____.

134. RUN SOMETHING BY SOMEONE.

Example:
A. Has Michele told you what he's planning for the meeting next week?
B. Yeah, he ran some ideas by me yesterday.

Meaning:
This phrase means to share ideas about something.

Now make your sentences.
1. _____.
2. _____.
3. _____.

135 DAYS ARE NUMBERED.

Meaning:
Days are numbered is used to say that someone or something will die, fail, or end soon.

Examples:
1. The doctors have told me that my *days are numbered.*
2. The *days of large gas-guzzling cars are numbered.*

Now make your sentences.
1. _____.
2. _____.
3. _____.

TREASURE BOX:9

Try to feel the language when you speak it. There is more than learning the phrases, grammar and vocabulary. You have to immerse yourself in the language by listening and mimicking to make it more natural when you speak.

136. TAKE ME BACK.

Example:
Jilly: This *takes me back*, I haven't been to the seaside since I was a child.
Nicola: I haven't been for ages either.
Jilly: Tell you what, let's go on the pier and get some cotton candy.
Nicola: But that's for kids and it's pure sugar; it'll ruin your figure.
Jilly: I don't care, it was one of my favorite things to have when we came to the seaside.
Nicola: Well, if you're going to relive your childhood, I'm going to have to do the same.

Meaning:

If you say that something takes you back, you mean that it reminds you of a period of your past life and makes you think about it again.

Now make your sentences.

1. _____.
2. _____.
3. _____.

137. JUST THIS ONCE.

Meaning:

This expression is made to ask or make an exception.

Example:

A. I need to leave work early today. Is that possible? An hour early.

B. OK. Just this once.

A. Thanks.

B. Sure!

Now make your sentences.

1. _____.
2. _____.
3. _____.

138. CALL IN SICK

Meaning:

To telephone work or school to say you are ill and will not be there

Example:

I woke up with a terrible cold and had to call in sick last week.

Now make your sentences.
1. _____.
2. _____.
3. _____.

139. A WIN-WIN SITUATION.

Jason: We'll give you the order if you can guarantee delivery in three weeks.
Keith: If you confirm the order today, we'll deliver in two weeks.
Jason: If you can deliver in two weeks, that would give us a big advantage over our competitors.
Keith: We definitely can, our workers are very experienced and we have the latest equipment.
Jason: Looks like we've got a win-win situation here. You've got our order.
Keith: That's great. We'll start on it straight away.

Meaning::
A win-win situation is one in which an agreement is reached that is beneficial to both sides.

Now make your sentences.
1. _____.
2. _____.
3. _____.

140. FLAVOR OF THE MONTH

Example:
"A lot of celebrities are only famous for a short amount of time, and whoever is the flavor of the month right now may be forgotten in the nearest future."

Meaning:
Flavor of the month is used to describe someone or something that is temporarily popular.

Now make your sentences.

1. _____.
2. _____.
3. _____.

REVIEW: 7

Fill in the gaps with the right prepositions.

1. Actually, I'm thinking ……….. leaving the company.

2. Thank you……..agreeing to meet us at such short notice.

3. Fortunately, we succeeded……… meeting the deadline.

4. I don't believe ………taking too much notice of our competitors.

5. Let's just concentrate………….doing what we do best.

6. I don't blame him……………….starting up on his own.

7. I won't prevent you………….. going ahead if you want to.

8. I warned you …………. taking on too much work too quickly.

9. Success depends………being in the right place at the right time.

10. I'm looking for someone to take care of my baby. Can I rely……… you?

141. NOT THAT I KNOW OF.

Example:
Mei: Is Mrs. Johnson joining us for dinner?
Susie: Not that I know of.
Mei:I was hoping she would come with us.
Susie: Why?
Mei:I would like her to try some of our traditional Chinese foods.
Susie: That's very kind of you.

Meaning:
You say 'Not that I know of' when someone has asked you whether or not something is true and you think the answer is; 'no' but you cannot be sure because you do not know all the facts.

Now make your sentences.
1. _____.
2. _____.
3. _____.

142. AS FAR AS I CAN SEE.

Example:
A. Is it raining outside?
B. Not as far as I can see. But maybe it's just about to start.

Meaning:
We use this expression when we are not completely confident about information that we are giving.

Now make your sentences.
1. _____.
2. _____.
3. _____.

143. IF YOU MUST.

Example:
A. Do you mind if I open the window - it's stuffy in here.
B. If you must. But I've got a cold, so just for 10 minutes

Meaning:
We use this expression to say that someone can do something, but we perhaps prefer them not to do it.

Now make your sentences.

1. _____.
2. _____.
3. _____.

144. ROCK THE BOAT.

Meanings and examples:
It means to cause trouble by changing or trying to change
a situation that other people do not want to change.
a. Please don't **rock the boat**.
b. he system isn't perfect, but it's been this way for a long time and nobody
   wants to **rock the boat**.
This is an Idiomatic expression.

Now make your sentences.

1. _____.
2. _____.
3. _____.

145. SPEAK YOUR MIND.

Michelle Thanks so much for your hard work. I'm so impressed by your feedback. We got our sponsors now. We have won over several suppliers supporting us and everything. Good job, everyone.
Sam: That's part of our job. We're glad we helped.
Michelle: Good. And it's time to discuss how we should promote our key items. There's plenty of information in your handouts.
Now speak your minds.
Sam: We definitely need to choose Internet as a means of marketing. It's the current trend.
Michelle: That's right. We can create a promotion page with attractive banners, and so our company website can stay unchanged but we can still attract buyers.
Sam: Then the decisions are made. Let's do that.

Meaning:
Speak your mind - To say what you think about something very directly

Now make your sentences.
1. _____.
2. _____.
3. _____.

TREASURE BOX:10

> Be consistent with your study. Create a routine and work toward achieving
> your set goal. The moment you step aside from your routine, you may lose
> the ones you have learned.

146. THAT'S QUITE SOMETHING

Meaning:
We use this expression to show we are impressed by something special we have
seen or heard.

Example
A. My cousin started his own company and was a millionaire by the age of 20.
B. That's quite something, isn't it?

Now make your sentences.
1. _____.
2. _____.
3. _____.

147. AS THEY SAY...

Meaning:
We use this expression when we have used a proverb or saying or popular
quotation to indicate that what we said is not just our opinion..

Example:
A. I don't see how you will be able to travel around the world with just $500!
B. Where there's a will there's a way, as they say, I've got some ideas.

Now make your sentences.
1. _____.
2. _____.
3. _____.

148. PAIN IN THE NECK

Meaning:
A difficult or annoying thing or person.

Example:
This project is a pain in the neck.

Now make your sentences.
1. _____.
2. _____.
3. _____.

149. GIVE ME A BREAK

Meaning:
It is difficult to believe this is true or real.

Example:
You're going to run in tomorrow's marathon? Giveme a break!

Now make your sentences.
1. _____.
2. _____.
3. _____.

150. FROM THE HORSE'S MOUTH

Meaning:

If you get information about something from the horse's mouth, you get it from someone who isinvolved in it and knows a lot about it

Example:

I know it's true! I heard it straight from the horse's mouth!

Now make your sentences.

1. _____.
2. _____.
3. _____.

Fill in the gaps with the right prepositions.

1. Actually, I'm thinking …of…….. leaving the company.

2. Thank you …for… agreeing to meet us at such short notice.

3. Fortunately, we succeeded……in… meeting the deadline.

4. I don't believe ……in…taking too much notice of our competitors.

5. Let's just concentrate……on…….doing what we do best.

6. I don't blame him………for………starting up on his own.

7. I won't prevent you……from…….. going ahead if you want to.

8. I warned you ……against……. taking on too much work too quickly.

9. Success depends……on…being in the right place at the right time.

10. I'm looking for someone to take care of my baby. Can I rely……on… you?

151. MAKE A LONG STORY SHORT / CUT A LONG STORY SHORT

Meaning:
To leave out parts of a story to make it shorter or to bring a story to an end.

Example:
Andto make a long story short, Inever got back the money that I lent him.

Now make your sentences.
1. _____.
2. _____.
3. _____.

152. BITE OFF MORE THAN ONE CAN CHEW

Meaning:
To attempt something that exceeds one's capacity.

Example:
In trying to build a house by himself, my friend bit offmore than he could chew.

Now make your sentences.
1. _____.
2. _____.
3. _____.

153. BITE SOMEONE'S HEAD OFF.

Meaning:
To respond with anger or impatience to someone's question or comment:

Example:
He'll bite your head off if you ask for anything.

Now make your sentences.
1. _____.
2. _____.
3. _____.

154. UNTIL ONE IS BLUE IN THE FACE.

Example:
"The teacher kept telling the students to sit still until he was blue in the face, but they did not stop."

Meaning:
If a person does something until they are blue in the face, it means that they don't succeed, no matter how hard they try.

Now make your sentences.
1. _____.
2. _____.
3. _____.

155. WHY DON'T WE....?

Meaning:
When using this phrase you are inviting or giving the person you are talking to, an opinion to do something together.

Examples:
"Why don't we go bowling tonight?"
"Why don't we play a game of chess?"
"Why don't we test this before using it?"

Now make your sentences.
1. _____.
2. _____.
3. _____.

156. RAIN CHECK!!!

Example in conversation:
Jean: My brother and his family will be coming into town next week.

Joe: Is he the one who writes articles for the ABC Post?

Jean: Right, why don't you come over next Sunday to meet him.

Joe: I'd love to but I can't. Can you give me a rain check!!!

Jean: Sure, they'll be here for a week. So just let me know when you can come.

Joe: Ok! I will be very interested in seeing him.

Meaning:

If you say you will take a rain check on an offer or suggestion, you mean that you do not want to accept it straight away, but you might accept it at another time.

Now make your sentences.

1. _____.
2. _____.
3. _____.

157. IT'S TOO BAD THAT.....

Meaning:

'Too bad' means unfortunate or sad. When using it in a sentence you are expressing a concern or regret for what has taken place.

Examples:

"It's too bad that she lost her job."

"It's too bad that you have to go."

"It's too bad we will not be there on time.

Now make your sentences.

1. _____.
2. _____.
3. _____.

158. I AM ON TOP OF THAT.

Michelle: Renee, did you talk to our suppliers about our promotion details?

Renee: Yes, I did. I've asked them to insert fliers into the shipments to our customers too.

Michelle: Do you need someone to help you send messages to customers by email?

Renee: No thanks. That's my job. I am on top of that.

Michelle: Oh, and did you discuss the exhibitions we talked about last night with our channel?

Renee: Of course I did. And they've promised to help us.

Michelle: Wow, I'm impressed. You've improved a lot as a sales representative.

Meaning:

To be on top of something is to be able to control a situation.

Now make your sentences.

1. _____.
2. _____.
3. _____.

159. BE TORN

Example:

"I'm torn between going to sleep early tonight and watching a movie with my friends."

Meaning:

A person is torn if they have multiple options but can't decide what to do.

Now make your sentences.

1. _____.
2. _____.
3. _____.

160. IT LOOKS LIKE.....

Meaning:

1. You could be describing how something is similar or appears to be by the way it looks.

Example:
"It looks like a banana.

2. You can also use 'it looks like' to describe something that might be in the future.

Example:
"It looks like it's going to rain."

3. You can also use it to describe something in the present progressive tense.

Examples:
"It looks like they are leaving."
"It looks like he is waving to us."

Now make your sentences.
1. _____.
2. _____.
3. _____.

REVIEW: 8

Fill in the gaps with the right phrasal verbs.

1) The music and laughter gradually _____ as the procession moved off down the street.

   [a] hid away
   [b] faded away
   [c] ran away

2) The more you _____ from the shops, the less money you'll spend.

   [a] get away
   [b] go away
   [c] keep away

3) I had to _____ the presents in the bedroom, so that the children wouldn't find them.

   [a] put away
   [b] give away
   [c] hide away

4) She likes to keep things, even old things, rather than _____.

   [a] put them away
   [b] get away with
   [c] throw them away

5) I think of the new boy who _____ because he was being bullied.

   [a] gave away
   [b] kept away
   [c] ran away

6) Albert folded the newspaper neatly and _____.

    [a] put it away
    [b] keep it away
    [c] get it away

7) This man wanted to help them keep their land, not_____ from them.

    [a] put it way
    [b] take it away
    [c] keep it way

8) I'm not going to allow Anne to _____ an offensive remark like that.

    [a] keep away
    [b] get way
    [c] get away with

9) I had to _____. One way or another, I was going to leave Birmingham.

    [a] get away with
    [b] keep away
    [c] get away

10) You should always _____ from the kitchen.

    [a] take animals away
    [b] keep animals away
    [c] put animals away

161. BRING (OR COME) TO LIGHT

Example:
"After new evidence was brought to light, the banker was found guilty of stealing money."

Meaning:

This phrase means that something becomes public.
"bring to light" means that someone purposefully makes something public;
"come to light" means that something becomes public, but maybe by accident.

Now make your sentences.
1. _____.
2. _____.
3. _____.

162. OUT OF THIS WORLD.

Example:
"These cookies are out of this world!"

Meaning:
Out of this world is a term used to describe something that is amazing or impressive.

Now make your sentences.
1. _____.
2. _____.
3. _____.

163. THAT'S WHY........

Meanings:
'That's' = 'that is.' = 'because of this' or 'therefore.'
You say this when you are telling someone the reason for a situation.

Examples:
"That's why people admire you."
"That's why she appears so happy."
"That is why you lock your doors when you leave home."

Now make your sentences.

1. _____.
2. _____.
3. _____.

164. THROW THE BOOK AT SOMEONE.

Example:

"The judge threw the book at the man, sentencing him to 55 years in jail."

Meaning:

To throw the book at someone means to severely punish them.

Now make your sentences.

1. _____.
2. _____.
3. _____.

165. IT'S TIME TO.....

Meaning:

You are letting someone know that something is required to be done at the present time.

Examples:

"It's time to say goodbye."
"It's time to ask for a raise."
"It's time to decide what to do."
Try to make your sentences with this phrase.

Now make your sentences.

1. _____.
2. _____.
3. _____.

TREASURE BOX:11

> To become proficient or good in English you have to take responsibility and be active in acquiring it. How well you succeed is really up to you.

166. NOTHING TO WRITE HOME ABOUT.

Example:
"This restaurant's food is nothing to write home about."

Meaning:
Something is nothing to write home about if it is unmemorable and ordinary.

167. THE POINT IS THAT.........

Meaning:
This phrase means you are stating your opinion about what is actually happening.

Examples:
"The point is that we need this done today."
"The point is that snakes can be dangerous."
"The point is that leaving a baby alone in the car is not a good idea."

Now make your sentences.
1. _____.
2. _____.
3. _____.

168. I WAS MILES AWAY

Meaning:
We use this expression to say that we were thinking about something else.

Example:

A. ...and that's how you use the new computer system.

B. Sorry, could you explain that again. I was miles away.

Now make your sentences.

1. _____.
2. _____.
3. _____.

169. DRIVE SOMEONE CRAZY.

Also, **drive someone mad** or **bananas** or **bonkers** or **nuts** or **up the wall** etc.

Meaning:
To **annoy, irritate, bother, provoke.**

Example:
His habitual lateness drives me crazy

Now make your sentences.

1. _____.
2. _____.
3. _____.

170. JOIN THE CLUB

Meaning:
We use this expression to say that we are in the same situation as someone, or have had the same bad experience.

Example:

A. I got married when I was 21, and divorced at 25. I don't think I'll get married again.

B. Join the club. I'm much happier single.

Now make your sentences.

1. _____.

2. _____.

3. _____.

REVIEW: 8. ANSWER

Fill in the gaps with the right phrasal verbs.

1) The music and laughter gradually _____b_____ as the procession moved off down the street.

   [a]hid away
   [b]faded away
   [c]ran away

2) The more you _____c_____ from the shops, the less money you'll spend.

   [a]get away
   [b]go away
   [c]keep away

3) I had to _____c_____ the presents in the bedroom, so that the children wouldn't find them.

   [a]put away
   [b]give away
   [c]hide away

4) She likes to keep things, even old things, rather than _____c_____.

   [a]put them away
   [b]get away with
   [c]throw them away

5) I think of the new boy who _____c_____ because he was being bullied.

   [a]gave away
   [b]kept away
   [c]ran away

6) Albert folded the newspaper neatly and _____a_____.

[a]put it away
[b]keep it away
[c]get it away

7) This man wanted to help them keep their land, not _____b_____ from them.

[a]put it way
[b]take it away
[c]keep it way

8) I'm not going to allow Anne to _____c_____ an offensive remark like that.

[a]keep away
[b]get way
[c]get away with

9) I had to _____c_____. One way or another, I was going to leave Birmingham.

[a]get away with
[b]keep away
[c]get away

10) You should always _____b_____ from the kitchen.

[a]take animals away
[b]keep animals away
[c]put animals away

171. I'M ALL EARS

Meaning:
We use this expression to say we are keen to listen to someone tell us something.

Example:

A. Have you heard what Jerome said to Cindy?

B. No. I'm all ears.

I'm all ears = I'm listening.

Now make your sentences.

1. _____.
2. _____.
3. _____.

172. TO BE HONEST.

Meaning:

We use this expression to introduce our real opinion about something - often when this is negative.

Example:

A. How's your new job?

B. To be honest, I'm finding it quite difficult at the moment.

A. I expect you'll settle in soon enough.

Now make your sentences.

1. _____.
2. _____.
3. _____.

173. I'LL TAKE YOUR WORD FOR IT.

Meaning:

We use this expression to say that we trust and believe someone about something. Often it implies that we do not want to do something that we think is negative.

Example:

A. Touch this, it's really hot!

B. No thanks. I'll take your word for it.

Now make your sentences.

1. _____.
2. _____.
3. _____.

174. I WOULDN'T COUNT ON IT.

Meaning:

We use this expression when we think that something is unlikely to happen.

Example:

A. Will Eric be at the party?
B. I wouldn't count on it. He never comes out.

Now make your sentences.

1. _____.
2. _____.
3. _____.

175. LIGHT A FIRE UNDER SOMEONE

Example:

"The manager lit a fire under his team by telling them that they must finish their work in only two hours, or they would not receive their bonus money."

Meaning:

If you light a fire under someone, you get them to work faster and harder.

Now make your sentences.

1. _____.
2. _____.
3. _____.

Live and breathe English.
Language is like a living thing! It breathes, it moves, it grows, it changes. It is dynamic! When you spend time living a language, it comes to you more naturally like it does to children.

176. CUT FROM THE SAME CLOTH.

Example:
"Even though we're not brothers, people always tell my friend and me that we're cut from the same cloth."

Meaning:
Cut from the same cloth is used to describe things that are very similar.

Now make your sentences.
1. _____.
2. _____.
3. _____.

177. GIVE IT A REST.

Meaning:
We use this expression to tell someone to stop talking about something.

Meaning:
A. Jackie's parents gave Jackie a laptop, and they gave her an MP3 player.
B. Give it a rest about Jackie, will you! I don't want to hear about her any more.

Now make your sentences.
1. _____.
2. _____.
3. _____.

178. WHAT ARE THE CHANCES OF.........

Meaning:
You can use this when you are wondering **how often** or **in what case** would something happen.

Examples:
"What are the chances of it raining today?"
"What are the chances of winning the lottery?"
Or
Change the word 'the' with 'your' or 'our' you can ask what the chances 'personally' that something will happen.

Examples:
"What are your chances of improving?"
"What are our chances of working together?"

Now make your sentences.
1. _____.
2. _____.
3. _____.

179. THERE'S NO NEED TO ....

Meaning:
This expression means that the action does not need to take place.

Examples:
"There's no need to worry."
"There's no need to be upset."

Now make your sentences.
1. _____.
2. _____.
3. _____.

180. IT TAKES ....

Meaning:
You are letting someone know how long it will take to do a particular thing.

Examples:
"It takes one hour to get there."
"It takes years to learn to play guitar."

Now make your sentences.
1. _____.
2. _____.
3. _____.

REVIEW: 9

Choose the right prepositions, particles, multi-word verbs or phrasal verbs to fill in the gaps.

1) My friend Sarah has missed the last bus. I will put her _____for the weekend

   [a] up
   [b] by
   [c] off
   [d] away

2) Because of bad weather we have asked the boss to put _____ he meeting until Monday.

   [a] off
   [b] up
   [c] away
   [d] by

3) Wait a minute, I'm coming. I've just to put the car _____

   [a] off
   [b] up
   [c] by
   [d] away

4) I've heard that Tommy is putting _____ $40 every month to buy a new bike.

   [a] away
   [b] by
   [c] up
   [d] off

5) I have looked _____ my mobile phone in my office, in the car, under the bed but I can't find it anywhere.

[a] up
[b] after
[c] back
[d] for

6) Look _____ and tell me I'm not dreaming, I've seen an alien behind us.

[a] back
[b] up
[c] for
[d] after

7) Many people keep hens to supply eggs. But like all animals, looking _____ chickens takes an effort.

[a] up
[b] after
[c] for
[d] back

8) You have misspelled the words 'dumbbell' and 'mischievous'. You had better look them _____ in a dictionary.

[a] up
[b] for
[c] back
[d] after

9) During the storm, the captain couldn't _____ the dangerous reefs and the ship sank.

[a] fell through
[b] gave up
[c] came across

[d] took up

[e] make out

10) All my plans _____ when I found out that it was not possible to get a loan to restore the old mill.

[a] make out

[b] fell through

[c] gave up

[d] came across

[e] took up

11) The other day, I _____ an old friend of mine. I hadn't seen him since he got married.

[a] gave up

[b] took up

[c] fell through

[d] make out

[e] came across

12) Peter _____

[a] gave up

[b] came across

[c] make out

[d] fell through

[e] took up

13) learning Mandarin two years ago, but after a few lessons he _____.

[a] came across

[b] gave up

[c] make out

[d] fell through

[e] took up

Are the phrases correct or incorrect?

14) After the party the house was a real mess. It took me five hours to **tidy up it.**

    [a] incorrect
    [b] correct

15) At the end of the day we **rode** to the stable **back.**

    [a] incorrect
    [b] correct

16) As I was walking through the forest a deer **ran past** me and quickly disappeared.

    [a] correct
    [b] incorrect

17) Children, it's late. **Put** your toys **away.**

    [a] correct
    [b] incorrect

18) and **put** your pajamas **on.**

    [a] correct
    [b] incorrect

181. THERE IS SOMETHING WRONG WITH....

Meaning:
You are informing someone that there is something not right or out of the ordinary.

Examples:
"There is something wrong with my laptop."
"There is something wrong with my car."

Now make your sentences.

1. _____.
2. _____.
3. _____.

182. LAND ON ONE'S FEET.

Example:

"After getting fired from his job, he landed on his feet by partnering with a friend and starting a new business."

Meaning:

If a person lands on their feet, it means that they have success after experiencing a time of difficulty or setback.

Now make your sentences.

1. _____.
2. _____.
3. _____.

183. BURY THE HATCHET.

Example:

"Let's bury the hatchet and stop fighting with each other."

Meaning:

If people bury the hatchet, that means they make peace with each other.

Now make your sentences.

1. _____.
2. _____.
3. _____.

184. NOT IN A MILLION YEARS.

Meaning:
We use this expression to say that we will never do something or that something will never happen.

Example:
A. Eric, do you think you'll ever work in China again.
B. Not in a million years.

Now make your sentences.
1. _____.
2. _____.
3. _____.

185. NOT TO MY KNOWLEDGE.

Meaning:
We use this expression to say that we think something is not true or has not happened as far as we know.

Example:
A. Is there a bank around here?
B. Not to my knowledge. I think there's one nearer the center, though.

Now make your sentences.
1. _____.
2. _____.
3. _____.

186. IN ALL LIKELIHOOD

Meaning:
We use this expression to say that something is probably true or going to happen.

Example:
A. When will the new building be finished?
B. In all likelihood it will open next month.

Now make your sentences.
1. _____.
2. _____.
3. _____.

187. IT'S VERY KIND OF YOU TO........

This phrase means that you appreciated or welcomed what someone has done or said.

Here are some **examples:**
"It's very kind of you to offer me the job."
"It's very kind of you to invite us."

Now make your sentences.
1. _____.
2. _____.
3. _____.

188. FROM NOW ON....

Meaning:
We use this expression to say that something will begin now and continue into the future - probably forever..

Example:
A. From now on you won't be allowed to answer personal emails at work.
B. **Why** not?
A. That's what the management has decided.

Now make your sentences.

1. _____.
2. _____.
3. _____.

189. SQUARE MEAL.

Examples:
1. After eating a square meal and sleeping for eight hours, I felt refreshed and full of energy.
2. Most supermodels don't look like they've had a square meal in their life.

Meaning:
A square meal is simply a meal that is enjoyable to eat and healthy.

Now make your sentences.

1. _____.
2. _____.
3. _____.

190. WE ENDED UP.........

Meaning:
It is often used to describe an action that was different from a plan or intention.

Example:
A: How was your dinner date last night?
B: We couldn't agree on a restaurant so we ended up eating at home.

Now make your sentences.

1. _____.
2. _____.
3. _____.

REVIEW: 9. ANSWER

Choose the right prepositions, particles, multi-word verbs or phrasal verbs to fill the gaps.

1) My friend Sarah has missed the last bus. I will put her ____up____for the weekend

   [a] up
   [b] by
   [c] off
   [d] away

2) Because of bad weather we have asked the boss to put ____off_____ he meeting until Monday.

   [a] off
   [b] up
   [c] away
   [d] by

3) Wait a minute, I'm coming. I've just to put the car ___away_____

   [a] off
   [b] up
   [c] by
   [d] away

4) I've heard that Tommy is putting _____away____ $40 every month to buy a new bike.

   [a] away
   [b] by
   [c] up
   [d] off

5) I have looked _____for_____ my mobile phone in my office, in the car, under the bed but I can't find it anywhere.

[a] up
[b] after
[c] back
[d] for

6) Look _____back_____ and tell me I'm not dreaming, I've seen an alien behind us.

[a] back
[b] up
[c] for
[d] after

7) Many people keep hens to supply eggs. But like all animals, looking _____after_____ chickens takes an effort.

[a] up
[b] after
[c] for
[d] back

8) You have misspelled the words 'dumbbell' and 'mischievous'. You had better look them _____up_____ in a dictionary.

[a] up
[b] for
[c] back
[d] after

9) During the storm, the captain couldn't _____make out_____ the dangerous reefs and the ship sank.

[a] fell through
[b] gave up
[c] came across

[d] took up

[e] make out

10) All my plans ____fell through____ when I found out that it was not possible to get a loan to restore the old mill.

[a] make out

[b] fell through

[c] gave up

[d] came across

[e] took up

11) The other day, I ___came across____ an old friend of mine. I hadn't seen him since he got married.

[a] gave up

[b] took up

[c] fell through

[d] make out

[e] came across

12) Peter _____took up___

[a] gave up

[b] came across

[c] make out

[d] fell through

[e] took up

13) learning Mandarin two years ago, but after a few lessons he _____gave up___.

[a] came across

[b] gave up

[c] make out

[d] fell through

[e] took up

Are the phrases correct or incorrect?

14) After the party the house was a real mess. It took me five hours to **tidy up it.**

    [a] incorrect

15) At the end of the day we **rode** to the stable **back.**

    [a] incorrect

16) As I was walking through the forest a deer **ran past** me and quickly disappeared.

    [a] correct

17) Children, it's late. **Put** your toys **away.**

    [a] correct

18) and **put** your pajamas **on.**

    [a] correct

191. KICK BACK.

Meaning:
This phrasal verb means to relax and enjoy yourself

Examples:
1. After work, he likes to kick back and watch some TV.
2. I spent the weekend just kicking back.

Now make your sentences.
1. _____.
2. _____.
3. _____.

192. CUT IT OUT.

Example:

"Cut it out! I'm trying to talk on the phone, and you are being very noisy!"

Meaning:

If you tell someone to cut it out, you are telling them to stop doing something.

Now make your sentences.
1. _____.
2. _____.
3. _____.

193. HAVE WIND AT ONE'S BACK

Example:

"The basketball player had the wind at his back and scored the winning basket."

Meaning:

If a person has the wind at their back, it means that they are having success and things are going smoothly and easily for them.

Now make your sentences.
1. _____.
2. _____.
3. _____.

194. GUT FEELING.

Meaning:

Gut feeling is a strong belief about someone or something

Example:

I have a gut feeling that the relationship won't last

Now make your sentences.

1. _____.
2. _____.
3. _____.

195. IT STRIKES ME....

Meaning:
We use this expression to introduce our impression or opinion of something.

Example:
A. Do you like Jerry?
B. Yes, he strikes me as a very talented person.

Now make your sentences.

1. _____.
2. _____.
3. _____.

TREASURE BOX:13

Become an English language chef, a charismatic one! Cook English in your brain, not when you are speaking. You may think a situation up in your Language and change it into English in many possible ways. Doing so will prepare you and help you connect when you need to.

196. AS WHITE AS A GHOST

Meaning:
This expression is mainly used to describe the way people look when they are frightened. When people are frightened of something, their facial skin turns white.

Example:
What happened to you? You are as white as a ghost.

Now make your sentences.

1. _____.
2. _____.
3. _____.

197. EVERY STEP OF THE WAY

Meaning:

If you help somebody every step of the way, you help them continuously.

Example:

I had a tough time finding a good job after finishing my studies. Fortunately for me, my parents supported me every step of the way.

Now make your sentences.

1. _____.
2. _____.
3. _____.

198. COME TO THINK OF IT.

Meaning:

You use the expression when you have suddenly realized something.
Come to think of it = I just remembered.

Example:

Come to think of it, I know someone who can help.

Now make your sentences.

1. _____.
2. _____.
3. _____.

199. IN THAT CASE

Example:
Me: Can I have a Guinness, please?
Bartender: I'm sorry, we run out of Guinness.
Me: In that case, I'll have a can of Chiba beer.
Bartender: Here you go!

Meaning:
We use this expression to give a suggestion for option or alternative for something that happened.

Now make your sentences.
1. _____.
2. _____.
3. _____.

200. THROW IN THE TOWEL.

Example:
A: "The boxing match is great."
B: "One guy is really getting beat up."
A: "Do you think he's going to give up?"
B: "He's not going to throw in the towel; they rarely do that these days."

Meaning:
This phrase means to give up or quit doing something.

Now make your sentences.
1. _____.
2. _____.
3. _____.

REVIEW: 10

Choose the best from A to D that matches the **Underlined** word or phrase.

1. "She's in the kitchen. I'll go get her. Can you stay on the line?" said Lisa to the caller.

    (A) remain
    (B) stop
    (C) hang
    (D) settle

2. "Let's head back to base. It's getting dark," said Charles to the rest of his hiking group.

    (A) revisit
    (B) return
    (C) revert
    (D) resume

3. The police pursued the runaway car until it stopped because it ran out of fuel.

    (A) chased after
    (B) chased off
    (C) get off
    (D) climbed on

4. While Catherine loved the opera, her boyfriend fell asleep in a matter of minutes.

    (A) hung up
    (B) got away
    (C) let down
    (D) dozed off

5. "What is going on here? Who are all these people?" said Carl when he got home early to find his daughter having a party.

   (A) starting
   (B) stirring
   (C) happening
   (D) commencing

6. "I wonder if Judy is going to show up at tonight's party," said Raymond.

   (A) appear
   (B) perform
   (C) boast
   (D) act

7. "Somebody broke into the vault and took all the money!" said an alarmed Dane.

   (A) ruptured
   (B) stabbed
   (C) penetrated
   (D) pierced

8. "Libby got in at 9 this morning. He wasn't late, for a change," said Libby's boss.

   (A) attended
   (B) registered
   (C) reported
   (D) arrived

9. "Stop making up excuses every time you come in late. Just get here on time," said Jenny's boss.

   (A) changing
   (B) inventing
   (C) deceiving
   (D) lying

10. I think you <u>left out</u> my name, Miss Lynn," said Mina to her form teacher.

   (A) lost
   (B) missed
   (C) ignored
   (D) neglected

201. IT NEVER CROSSED MY MIND.

Meaning:
We use this expression to say that we didn't even think of something.

Example:
A. Weren't you worried about the parachute not opening when you jumped?
B. It never crossed my mind. I knew everything would be all right.

Now make your sentences.
1. _____.
2. _____.
3. _____.

202. READ MY LIPS!

Meaning:
This is a slightly impolite way of telling someone to listen to what you are saying.

Example:
Read my lips. You're not having any more ice-cream.

Now make your sentences.
1. _____.
2. _____.
3. _____.

203. FLY OFF THE HANDLE

Example:
"I know you weren't happy, but you should never **fly off the handle** like you did."

Meaning:
If a person flies off the handle, it means that they quickly lose their temper and become very angry.

Now make your sentences.
1. _____.
2. _____.
3. _____.

204. AS FAR AS I CAN SEE...

Meaning:
We use this expression when we are not completely confident about information that we are giving

Example:
A. Is it raining outside?
B. Not as far as I can see. But maybe it's just about to start.

Now make your sentences.
1. _____.
2. _____.
3. _____.

205. BOTTOM OF THE BARREL

Example:
"Everything that this store sells is the bottom of the barrel, and it isn't worth buying."

Meaning:
Something can be described as being the bottom of the barrel if it is not a good quality.

Now make your sentences.
1. _____.
2. _____.
3. _____.

206. HAVE TWO LEFT FEET.

Example:
"She is not a good dancer, and has always had two left feet."

Meaning:
If a person has two left feet, that means they are not good at dancing.

Now make your sentences.
1. _____.
2. _____.
3. _____.

207. ON AN EMPTY STOMACH.

MEANING:
This phrase means you have not eaten for some time.

Examples:
1. Take this medication on an empty stomach.
2. He left home early this morning on an empty stomach.

Now make your sentences.
1. _____.
2. _____.
3. _____.

208. MY TAKE ON IT.

Meaning:
We use this expression to give our opinion or viewpoint on a subject.

Example:
A. Why do you think the team is doing so badly?
B. Well, my take on it is that the players haven't played together long enough yet.

Now make your sentences.
1. _____.
2. _____.
3. _____.

209. A LOAD OF RUBBISH / A BUNCH OF GARBAGE.

Meaning:
We use this expression to say that we think something is not true, or it is useless.

Example:
A. Did you like the movie?
B. No. It was a load of rubbish.

Now make your sentences.
1. _____.
2. _____.
3. _____.

210. DAY IN, DAY OUT.

Meaning:
We use this expression to talk about something that is repetitive and probably negative or boring.

Example:

A. How are you getting on with your job?

B. Not so good. I do the same things day in, day out. It's very boring.

Now make your sentences.

1. _____.
2. _____.
3. _____.

REVIEW: 10. ANSWER

Choose the best from A to D that matches the **Underlined** word or phrase.

1. "She's in the kitchen. I'll go get her. Can you stay on the line?" said Lisa to the caller.

   (A) remain
   (B) stop
   (C) hang
   (D) settle

2. "Let's head back to base. It's getting dark," said Charles to the rest of his hiking group.

   (A) revisit
   (B) return
   (C) revert
   (D) resume

3. The police pursued the runaway car until it stopped because it ran out of fuel.

   (A) chased after
   (B) chased off
   (C) get off
   (D) climbed on

4. While Catherine loved the opera, her boyfriend fell asleep in a matter of minutes.

   (A) hung up
   (B) got away
   (C) let down
   (D) dozed off

5. "What is <u>going on</u> here? Who are all these people?" said Carl when he got home early to find his daughter having a party.

   (A) starting
   (B) stirring
   (C) happening
   (D) commencing

6. "I wonder if Judy is going to <u>show up</u> at tonight's party," said Raymond.

   (A) appear
   (B) perform
   (C) boast
   (D) act

7. "Somebody <u>broke into</u> the vault and took all the money!" said an alarmed Dane.

   (A) ruptured
   (B) stabbed
   (C) penetrated
   (D) pierced

8. "Libby <u>got in</u> at 9 this morning. He wasn't late, for a change," said Libby's boss.

   (A) attended
   (B) registered
   (C) reported
   (D) arrived

9. "Stop <u>making up</u> excuses every time you come in late. Just get here on time," said Jenny's boss.

   (A) changing
   (B) inventing
   (C) deceiving
   (D) lying

10. I think you <u>left out</u> my name, Miss Lynn," said Mina to her form teacher.

   (A) lost
   (B) missed
   (C) ignored
   (D) neglected

211. THAT'S NEWS TO ME.

Meaning:
We use this expression to say that we didn't know something.

Example:
A. My office is going to be painted next week, so we'll be sharing your office for a week.
B. That's news to me. Nobody told me.

Now make your sentences.
1. _____.
2. _____.
3. _____.

212. YOU WON'T REGRET IT.

Meaning:
We use this expression to say that someone will benefit from trusting us or our opinions. It is common after asking for a favor

Example:
A. So, you would like us to offer you a job here?
B. Yes, sir. I'm good with people. You won't regret it.

Now make your sentences.
1. _____.
2. _____.
3. _____.

213. IT'S A MUST.

Meaning:
We use this expression to recommend highly something, especially tourist sites or activities..

Example:
A. I'm wondering about visiting Kyoto - what do you think?
B. It's a must. You'll love it.

Now make your sentences.
1. _____.
2. _____.
3. _____.

214. DAWN ON SOMEONE.

Meaning:
This phrase means, to realize something.

Example:
It dawned on me that I had left my books at home.

Now make your sentences.
1. _____.
2. _____.
3. _____.

215. CAPITALIZE ON....

Meaning:
This phrase means to take advantage of something.

Example:
Let's capitalize on this opportunity.

Now make your sentences.

1. _____.
2. _____.
3. _____.

TREASURE BOX:14

Think of English as more of an art than a science. Many people study English as if it were a math or science. They often feel they are trying to solve a problem. Yes, you can study rules, but there are often more exceptions to the rules than there are rules.

216. "HAVE A FINGER IN EVERY PIE!!!

Jasmine: Kenny, how can I get promoted?
Kenny: You've got to get involved in things around here.
Jasmine: What do you mean?
Kenny: Act like Clint.
Jasmine: But he **has his finger in every pie.**
Kenny: Exactly. All of the managers see him, so he's bound to get promoted.
Jasmine: I'll give it a try. I've got nothing to lose but only a promotion to win.

Meaning:
This phrase means to have an interest in or be involved in everything"

Now make your sentences.

1. _____.
2. _____.
3. _____.

217. HAVE SEEN BETTER DAYS.

Example:
"This part of town has seen better days, but it is no longer a nice place to live in."

Meaning:
If a person, place, or thing has seen better days, that means it used to better than it is now.

Now make your sentences.
1. _____.
2. _____.
3. _____.

218. LAY A FINGER ON SOMEONE

Example:
"If you lay a finger on my little brother, I'll hit you!"

Meaning:
To lay a finger on someone means to hurt them.

Now make your sentences.
1. _____.
2. _____.
3. _____.

219. GET ONE'S HANDS DIRTY

Example:
"When a lot of employees suddenly quit, the CEO knew she had to leave her nice office and get her hands dirty."

Meaning:
This phrase means that someone does hard and usually unpleasant work.

Now make your sentences.
1. _____.
2. _____.
3. _____.

220. JUST A THOUGHT

Meaning:

We use this expression to say we have just had a good idea.

Example:

A. I don't know when I'm going to have time to go shopping.

B. Just a thought. Why don't you go online and get it all delivered?

A. Yes! I guess that's what I'm going to do, thanks!

B. Sure!

Now make your sentences.

1. _____.
2. _____.
3. _____.

REVIEW: 11

Fill in the blanks with phrases from the box below. Each phrase can only be used once.

adds up to, hung up on, snap out of,
get on with, went up against, keep out of,
wake up in, check in on, cut down on,
coming out on

1. "Your father and your uncle are in a heated debate about the ownership of the house. You best _____ it," said Betty to her son.

2. We need to _____ our expenses as the prices of goods are going up.

3. "Now that everyone is finally here, let's _____ it," said the impatient manager.

4. Samson was surprised to _____ his room. The last thing he remembers is passing out on the street.

5. It was just their luck that in their first dance off, they are _____ last year's champions.

6. "That rude receptionist _____ me while I was in mid-sentence," said an agitated Mrs. Stephen

7. "Everything _____ $130.24. We accept credit cards as well, sir," said the waiter to Mr. Mason.

8. "Eddie Larson, are you daydreaming in my class again? Well, _____ it!" warned Mrs. Virginia.

9. "I will _____ you tomorrow morning to see if you are ready to be discharged," said the friendly doctor to Cindy.

10. "My results are _____ Friday. I'm so excited and nervous at the same time," said Kelly.

221. YOU'LL BE LUCKY.

Meaning:

We use this expression to say that we think something is not likely to happen.

Example:

A. I'd like to leave early on Friday.

B. You'll be lucky. Our boss never lets anyone go home one minute before 5 o'clock.

Now make your sentences.

1. _____.
2. _____.
3. _____.

222. I'M THE ONE WHO

Meaning:

We use this expression to say that I am the person who is in charge.

Example:

A. Since we're going to Kyoto by road tomorrow. Why don't we leave before lunch?

B. Well, I'm the one who's driving, so I'd prefer to go later when there's less traffic.

Now make your sentences.

1. _____.
2. _____.
3. _____.

223. I'M NOT SAYING...

Meaning:

We use this expression to soften a negative point that we are introducing.

Example:

A. I think we need a new computer like the one we saw in the catalog.

B. I'm not saying it's expensive. I just think we could spend the money on something else

Now make your sentences.

1. _____.
2. _____.
3. _____.

224. REDUCE SOMEONE TO TEARS

Meaning:

To cause a person to cry through insults, frustration, and belittling.

Example:

He scolded her so much that she was reduced to tears
by the end of the meeting.

Now make your sentences.

1. _____.
2. _____.
3. _____.

225. I DON'T KNOW OFFHAND.

Meaning:

We use this expression to say we don't know something and need to check before you can give information.

Example:

A. Is Los Angeles more or less than ten hours behind Japan?

B. I don't know offhand. I think it's written on the map in the front of my diary, though.

Now make your sentences.

1. _____.
2. _____.
3. _____.

TREASURE BOX:15

Don't hold on to your dictionary too tightly. Your top priority in learning English should be to think in English and to connect in a conversation.

226. WHERE THERE'S A WILL...

Meaning:
We use this expression to say that something is possible if you really want to do it.
It's short for: where there's a will, there's a way..

Example:
A. Do you think I can still learn and play the piano?
B. Sure, where there's a will...

Now make your sentences.

1. _____.
2. _____.
3. _____.

227. SHOOT THE BREEZE.

Example:
"While I was waiting for my friend, I stood outside his office and shot the breeze with some other people."

Meaning:
If you shoot the breeze with someone, it means you chat, or casually talk, with him or her.

Now make your sentences.

1. _____.
2. _____.
3. _____.

228. SOMETHING ALONG THOSE LINES

Meaning:

We use this expression to say that the other person's idea is basically right.

Example:

I can't remember exactly what he said but it was something along those lines.

Now make your sentences.

1. _____.
2. _____.
3. _____.

229. GET WIND OF

Meaning:

If you get wind of something, it means you hear about it.

Example:

I don't want the press to get wind of our plans at this stage.

Now make your sentences.

1. _____.
2. _____.
3. _____.

230. IT'S NOT THE END OF THE WORLD

Meaning:

We use this expression to say that something is not too serious or negative. It's commonly used to reassure someone when something has gone wrong..

Example:

A. Oh no! We've missed the train.

B. Don't worry - it's not the end of the world. There's another one in an hour.

Now make your sentences.

1. _____.
2. _____.
3. _____.

REVIEW: 11. ANSWER

Fill in the blanks with phrases from the box below. Each phrase can be used only once.

adds up to, hung up on, snap out of,
get on with, went up against, keep out of,
wake up in, check in on, cut down on,
coming out on

1. "Your father and your uncle are in a heated debate about the ownership of the house. You better ____keep out of____ it," said Betty to her son.

2. We need to ____cut down on____ our expenses as the prices of goods are going up.

3. "Now that everyone is finally here, let's ____get on with____ it," said the impatient manager.

4. Samson was surprised to ____wake up in____ his room. The last thing he remembers is passing out on the street.

5. It was just their luck that in their first dance off, they _went up against_____ last year's champions.

6. "That rude receptionist ____hung up on____ me while I was in mid-sentence," said an agitated Mrs. Stephen

7. "Everything __adds up to_____ $130.24. We accept credit cards as well, sir," said the waiter to Mr. Mason.

8. "Eddie Larson, are you daydreaming in my class again? Well, __snap out of_____ it!" warned Mrs. Virginia.

9. "I will _check in on_____ you tomorrow morning to see if you are ready to be discharged," said the friendly doctor to Cindy.

10. "My results are __coming out on_____ Friday. I'm so excited and nervous at the same time," said Kelly.

231. MAKE UP ONE'S MIND'

Meaning:
If you **make up your mind**, you make a decision.

Example:
She made up her mind to look for a new job.

Now make your sentences.
1. _____.
2. _____.
3. _____.

232. AT THIS RATE.

Meaning:
We use this expression to say that something will or won't happen if the present situation continues. It is often, but not always, negative.

Example:
A. It looks like you're making good progress with the paperwork.
B. Yes. We'll have everything finished by lunchtime at this rate.

Now make your sentences.
1. _____.
2. _____.
3. _____.

233. IT REMAINS TO BE SEEN.

Meaning:
We use this expression to say we don't know something yet. Often it expresses doubt.

Example:

A. So you eventually invested in that new software?

B. Yes, but whether it will make a big difference to our workremains to be seen.

A. Well, let's wait and see

Now make your sentences.

1. _____.
2. _____.
3. _____.

234. DRINK THE KOOL-AID

Example:

"His company has a lot of problems, but he drank the Kool-Aid and thinks it is fantastic."

Meaning:

If someone drinks the Kool-Aid, it means they believe something without questioning it. It is usually used to describe someone in a negative way.

Now make your sentences.

1. _____.
2. _____.
3. _____.

235. THANKS A BUNCH!

Meaning:

We use this expression ironically when we are not very happy about something..

Example:

A. Have you seen my sandwich?

B. Ah! I found one on the table so I threw it away. I thought you had finished.

A. Thanks a bunch! That was my lunch.

Now make your sentences.

1. _____.
2. _____.
3. _____.

TREASURE BOX:16

Stop translating new words you hear directly into your native language in the middle of conversations. Our brains slow down when we are constantly translating English to and from our language.

236. DYED-IN-THE-WOOL

Meaning:
If you describe someone as dyed-in-the-wool, you mean they have very strong opinions and will not change.

Example:
My uncle was a dyed-in-the-wool farmer. He wouldn't change for anything.

Now make your sentences.

1. _____.
2. _____.
3. _____.

237. THIRD TIME LUCKY

Meaning:
We use this expression to sound hopeful after two negative or unlucky experiences.

Example:
A. I've taken my driving test twice before. I failed both times.
B. Third time lucky.
A. I hope so.

Now make your sentences.

1. _____.
2. _____.
3. _____.

238. STILL GOING STRONG

Meaning:
We use this expression to say that someone or something is still very healthy, still doing well.

Example:
A. How's your grandfather nowadays?
B. He's 95 but still going strong.
A. That's good.

Now make your sentences.

1. _____.
2. _____.
3. _____.

239. WORK THINGS OUT.

Meaning:
We use this expression to talk about finding a solution to a problem.

Example:
A. I'm afraid I'm not happy with this room. I need a bigger one with internet access.
B. OK, sir. I am sure we can work things out for you.
A. Great, I'll appreciate it.

Now make your sentences.

1. _____.
2. _____.
3. _____.

240. BANG UP-TO-DATE.

Meaning:

We use this expression to say something is completely modern, current or informed about everything.

Example:

A. I check the news on the internet about four or five times a day.

B. Me too. In my job it's important to be bang up-to-date with what's happening.

Now make your sentences.

1. _____.
2. _____.
3. _____.

REVIEW: 12

Choose the word or phrase that means the same as the phrasal verb used.

1. He has gone through a lot over the past two years.

   a. has experienced
   b. has traveled
   c. has done

2. He mustered up enough to go to the horror film.

   a. have good grades
   b. gather courage
   c. make money

3. He gobbled up the turkey before I could have any.

   a. cooked
   b. threw away
   c. finished eating

4. He is going to have to face up to his past.

   a. accept
   b. explain
   c. forget

5. I would appreciate it if you could stick up for me the next time we see your mother.

   a. introduce
   b. help with the work
   c. defend

6. Let's put off that meeting to next Monday.

   a. postpone
   b. schedule
   c. arrange

7. Let's put David down. It'll be fun.

   a. invite
   b. influence
   c. criticize

8. I have a great program that weeds out unwanted files.

   a. replaces
   b. deletes
   c. finds

241. MAKE ONE'S BLOOD RUN COLD.

Example:
When I was home alone, I heard noises that made my blood run cold.

Meaning:
If something makes your blood run cold, then it really scares you.

Now make your sentences.
1. _____.
2. _____.
3. _____.

242. EAR TO THE GROUND.

Example:
The manager had her ear to the ground, and she knew how her employees were feeling.

Meaning:
If a person has their ear to the ground, that means they are aware of what is happening around them.

Now make your sentences.
1. _____.
2. _____.
3. _____.

243. THAT'S A LIKELY STORY.

Meaning:
We use this expression to say that we don't believe what someone has told us.

Example:
A. He said he couldn't come to school because he was helping the police with an investigation.
B. That's a likely story. He's probably just in bed sleeping.

Now make your sentences.
1. _____.
2. _____.
3. _____.

244. SWEEP SOMEONE OFF THEIR FEET

Meaning:
"My husband swept me off my feet ten years ago, on our first date."

Example:
If you sweep someone off their feet, that means they become very charmed by you and attracted to you.

Now make your sentences.

1. _____.
2. _____.
3. _____.

245. BREAK EVEN

Meaning:
To be having equal costs and income.

Example:
After years of investment the company finally was able to breakeven and it is hoping to make a profit soon.

Now make your sentences.

1. _____.
2. _____.
3. _____.

246. HAVE NOTHING TO DO WITH

1. To be irrelevant or unrelated.

Example:
Their visit has nothing to do with the holiday.
2. Avoid.

Example:
Dad insisted that we have nothing to do with the neighbors.

Now make your sentences.

1. _____.
2. _____.
3. _____.

247. ON SECOND THOUGHT

Meaning:

After having thought about something again.

Example:

On second thought we decided that it would be too expensive to fly, so we took a bus instead.

Now make your sentences.

1. _____ .
2. _____ .
3. _____ .

248. PAVE THE WAY FOR (SOMETHING OR SOMEONE)

Meaning:

To make it easier for something to happen or for someone to do something.

Example:

The space shuttle program helped pave the way for future programs.

Now make your sentences.

1. _____ .
2. _____ .
3. _____ .

249. REGARDLESS OF

Meaning:

Without being stopped or affected by (something)

Example:

He runs every day regardless of the weather because he wants to stay in shape.

Now make your sentences.

1. _____.
2. _____.
3. _____.

250. Take someone / something for granted

Meaning:
To use, accept, or treat in a careless or indifferent manner:

Example:
A marriage can be headed for trouble if either spouse begins to take the other for granted.

Now make your sentences.

1. _____.
2. _____.
3. _____.

REVIEW: 12. ANSWER

Choose the word or phrase that means the same as the phrasal verb used.

1. He has gone through a lot over the past two years.

    a. has experienced
    b. has traveled
    c. has done

2. He mustered up enough to go to the horror film.

    a. have good grades
    b. gather courage
    c. make money

3. He gobbled up the turkey before I could have any.

    a. cooked
    b. threw away
    c. finished eating

4. He is going to have to face up to his past.

    a. accept
    b. explain
    c. forget

5. I would appreciate it if you could stick up for me the next time we see your mother.

    a. introduce
    b. help with the work
    c. defend

6   Let's put off that meeting to next Monday.

   a.   postpone
   b.   schedule
   c.   arrange

7.   Let's put David down. It'll be fun.

   a.   invite
   b.   influence
   c.   criticize

8.   I have a great program that weeds out unwanted files.

   a.   replaces
   b.   deletes
   c.   finds

251. WHEN IT COMES TO...

Meaning:
As regards or concerning.

Example:
When it comes to renting or buying, you'll spend about the same amount

Now make your sentences.
1. _____.
2. _____.
3. _____.

252. TAKE INTO ACCOUNT

Meaning:
To remember to consider someone or something.

Example:
I'll try to take into account all the things that are important in a situation like this.

Now make your sentences.

1. _____.
2. _____.
3. _____.

253. WRIGGLE OUT OF

Meaning:

To avoid one's responsibility in some clever or dishonest way.

Example:

You are to blame and don't try to wriggle out of it!

Now make your sentences.

1. _____.
2. _____.
3. _____.

254. KEEP TRACK.

Meaning:

To be aware; keep informed:

Example:

I watch the news to keep track of current events.

Now make your sentences.

1. _____.
2. _____.
3. _____.

255. KEEP AFTER SOMEONE.

Meaning:

To tell someone again and again to do something.

Example:

My kids kept after me to quit smoking, so I finally did.

Now make your sentences.

1. _____.
2. _____.
3. _____.

TREASURE BOX:17

Try to understand the new word or phrase from context. The words and ideas around them should help you make a good guess. Pick up the clues such as the Subject and the action or verb and once you know the context of the discussion, you will be able to contribute and connect the dots.

256. TRACK DOWN

Meaning:

To follow successfully or to locate.

Example:

I've been trying to track down that book but haven't had any luck.

Now make your sentences.

1. _____.
2. _____.
3. _____.

257. WAVE ASIDE SOMETHING.

Meaning:

To refuse to consider or respond to something.

Example:

The officer waved aside my questions.

Now make your sentences.

1. _____.
2. _____.
3. _____.

258. SIZE SOMETHING OR SOMEONE UP.

Meaning:

To consider something or someone in order to form an opinion or conclusion.

Example:

She quickly sized up the situation and fled the scene.

Now make your sentences.

1. _____.
2. _____.
3. _____.

259. SHOOT THROUGH THE ROOF

Meaning:

This expression means to increase quickly or to become very angry

Examples:

1. My father went through the roof when he saw what I did to the car.
2. These days, prices for gasoline are going through the roof.

Now make your sentences.

1. _____.
2. _____.
3. _____.

260. BUSY AS A BEAVER OR BUSY AS A BEE.

Meaning:

Hardworking, very industrious.

Example:

With all her activities, Cecil is always busy as a bee.

Now make your sentences.

1. _____.
2. _____.
3. _____.

REVIEW: 13

Fill in the gaps with the right phrases.

1. When Paul's father passed away, Paul _____ the reigns of the family business.

    (A) took off
    (B) took away
    (C) took over
    (D) took down

2. In his attempt to take incredible pictures of the river, the photographer _____ the bridge into the water below.

    (A) fell off
    (B) flew off
    (C) dripped off
    (D) drifted off

3. Mike _____ his dad when it comes to interests: cars, war games and cooking.

    (A) goes after
    (B) follows after
    (C) takes after
    (D) trails after

4. Fortunately, no one was hurt in the _____ except for the shooter.

    (A) stand-off
    (B) shoot-out
    (C) meet-up
    (D) face-off

5. "_____ for your rights, women!" said the suffragette to the growing crowd.

   (A) Stand under
   (B) Stand over
   (C) Stand in
   (D) Stand up

6. Night guards caught Mr. Benson _____ his neighbor.

   (A) watching on
   (B) spying on
   (C) eavesdropping on
   (D) waiting on

7. "I've been framed. It's a _____ by the government!" the convict rambled on and on.

   (A) slip up
   (B) shake up
   (C) cover up
   (D) mix up

8. The private investigator _____ Mr. Goh's runaway daughter to a small village in Portugal.

   (A) tracked down
   (B) looked down
   (C) locked down
   (D) searched down

9. Meg _____ her headlights then exited the car, not noticing that her right tire had punctured.

   (A) turned away
   (B) turned into
   (C) turned about
   (D) turned off

10. "I cannot _____ with this anymore," said Dave's mum when she saw the mess the house was in.

(A) put in
(B) put up
(C) put off
(D) put out

261. AT LOGGERHEADS

Meaning:
In a state of strong disagreement

Example:
The twins were at loggerheads over who should take the larger room.

Now make your sentences.

1. _____.
2. _____.
3. _____.

262. SPLIT SECOND

Meaning:
An instant; a tiny period of time

Example:
The lightning struck, and in a split secondthe house burst into flames.

Now make your sentences.

1. _____.
2. _____.
3. _____.

263. GIVE AWAY,

Meaning:
To give as a present orto reveal a secret.

Example:
That remark gave away his real feelings.

Now make your sentences.
1. _____.
2. _____.
3. _____.

264. REFLECT (BACK) (UP) ON SOMEONE OR SOMETHING

Meaning:
To remember or think about someone or something. (Upon is formal and less commonly used than on.)

Example:
When I reflect back on the years I spent with my parents, I think I had a good childhood.

Now make your sentences.
1. _____.
2. _____.
3. _____.

265. MEDDLE WITH SOMEONE OR SOMETHING

Meaning:
To interfere with someone or something.

Example:
Please don't meddle with me. I am in a bad mood.

Now make your sentences.

1. _____.
2. _____.
3. _____.

266. TURN DOWN

Meanings and Examples:

1. To diminish the speed, volume, intensity, or flow of something by turning a dial:

Example: He turned down the TV so his roommate could study.

2. To reject or refuse someone or something:

Example: We turned them down because their offer was too low.

Now make your sentences.

1. _____.
2. _____.
3. _____.

267. GET INTO THE SWING.

Meaning:
To begin to fit into a routine etc.

Example:
After spending almost six months at the job, Ifinally get into the swing of things.

Now make your sentences.

1. _____.
2. _____.
3. _____.

268. GO WELL WITH.

Meaning:
Look good with, match.

Example:
This chair goes well with the rest of the furniture.

Now make your sentences.
1. _____.
2. _____.
3. _____.

269. DRESS UP

Meaning:
1. To put on one's best or fanciest clothing or dress relatively formally.

Example:
They were dressed up for the Easter parade.

2   To improve the appearance or impression of:
The presenter tried to dress up the uninteresting data.

Now make your sentences.
1. _____.
2. _____.
3. _____.

270. THROW AWAY

1. To get rid of something useless:
A. Is it all right to throw away these shoes?
B. No way! They are my favorites.
2. To fail to take advantage of:
    I threw away a chance to make a fortune last week.

Now make your sentences.

1. _____.
2. _____.
3. _____.

1. When Paul's father passed away, Paul ____C____ the reigns of the family business.

   (A) took off
   (B) took away
   (C) took over
   (D) took down

2. In his attempt to take incredible pictures of the river, the photographer _____A__ the bridge into the water below.

   (A) fell off
   (B) flew off
   (C) dripped off
   (D) drifted off

3. Mike _____C__ his dad when it comes to interests: cars, war games and cooking.

   (A) goes after
   (B) follows after
   (C) takes after
   (D) trails after

4. Fortunately, no one was hurt in the ____A____ except for the shooter.

   (A) stand-off
   (B) shoot-out
   (C) meet-up
   (D) face-off

5. "___D___ for your rights, women!" said the suffragette to the growing crowd.

   (A) Stand under
   (B) Stand over
   (C) Stand in
   (D) Stand up

6. Night guards caught Mr. Benson __B___ his neighbor.

   (A) watching on
   (B) spying on
   (C) eavesdropping on
   (D) waiting on

7. "I've been framed. It's a ___C___ by the government!" the convict rambled on and on.

   (A) slip up
   (B) shake up
   (C) cover up
   (D) mix up

8. The private investigator _____A__ Mr. Goh's runaway daughter to a small village in Portugal.

   (A) tracked down
   (B) looked down
   (C) locked down
   (D) searched down

9. Meg __D_____ her headlights then exited the car, not noticing that her right tire had punctured.

   (A) turned away
   (B) turned into
   (C) turned about
   (D) turned off

10. "I cannot ___B___ with this anymore," said Dave's mum when she saw the mess the house was in.

   (A) put in
   (B) put up
   (C) put off
   (D) put out

271. TAKE SOMETHING WITH A GRAIN OF SALT

Meaning:
To consider something to be not completely true or right.

Example:
I've read the article, which I take with a grain of salt

Now make your sentences.
1. _____.
2. _____.
3. _____.

272. HEAD FOR./DOWN/ BACK

Meaning:
To go in a specified direction or toward a specified place.

Examples:
i.   She turned around and headed (for) home.
ii. I hopped in the car and headed down the street.
iii. After lunch, we headed back to the office.

Now make your sentences.
1. _____.
2. _____.
3. _____.

273. SCRATCH YOUR HEAD.

Meaning:
To be confused about something and unable to understand the reason for it

Example:
His odd behavior left us all scratching our heads.

Now make your sentences.

1. _____.
2. _____.
3. _____.

274. OVER YOUR HEAD

Meaning:
Beyond your understanding or ability

Example:
The technical details were over my head.

Now make your sentences.

1. _____.
2. _____.
3. _____.

275. HAVE A HEAD FOR

Meaning:
To have an ability to understand or deal with something.

Example:
She's always had a head for business.

Now make your sentences.

1. _____.
2. _____.
3. _____.

TREASURE BOX:18

Don't try to write or read in the air or in your head while speaking. It will hinder you to follow the conversation.

276. GET IT THROUGH YOUR HEAD.

Meaning:
To accept or understand something.

Example:
He can't seem to get it through his head that I'm not interested in working with him.

Now make your sentences.

1. _____.
2. _____.
3. _____.

277. HAVE EYES IN THE BACK OF YOUR HEAD

Meaning:
When people are surprised that you have seen or noticed something that is behind you, they may say that you have eyes in the back of your head.

Example:
How did you know we were here? You must have eyes in the back of your head!

Now make your sentences.

1. _____.
2. _____.
3. _____.

278. HAVE AN EYE TO/TOWARD SOMETHING.

Meaning:

To have something in your thoughts as a goal or purpose

Example:

She has an eye to running the company in the near future.

Now make your sentences.

1. _____.
2. _____.
3. _____.

279. IN THE TWINKLE / BLINK OF AN EYE

Meaning:

In a very short time or very quickly

Example:

He was back in the twinkle of an eye.

Now make your sentences.

1. _____.
2. _____.
3. _____.

280. LAY/ SET EYES ON.

Meaning:

To see or look at someone or something.

Example:

We liked the house from the moment we set eyes on it.

Now make your sentences.

1. _____.
2. _____.
3. _____.

REVIEW: 14

Fill in the gaps with the best options.

1. "I can't _____ the feeling that I am being watched," said the actress to her friends.

   (A) shake at
   (B) shake off
   (C) shake down
   (D) shake away

2. The car _____ the poor puppy and then sped off quickly.

   (A) ran off
   (B) ran past
   (C) ran into
   (D) ran over

3. The guard _____ and let the nurse into the patient's room, not knowing it was the assassin in disguise.

   (A) stood over
   (B) stood back
   (C) stood aside
   (D) stood under

4. The story was _____ the eighteenth century and was about two lovebirds who were separated by their feuding families.

   (A) set down
   (B) set around
   (C) set off
   (D) set on

5. "I'm tired of people _____ on us. I want to make something out of myself," said Jack's oldest son, who is thinking of quitting school to go work.

   (A) looking for
   (B) looking between
   (C) looking after
   (D) looking down

6. Hellen's fiancé _____ with her money and passport, and left her stranded at the resort.

   (A) got off
   (B) drop off
   (C) took off
   (D) cut off

7. "Something _____. I have to go. Let's do this another time," said Linda before running out of the diner.

   (A) came up
   (B) came over
   (C) came off
   (D) came around

8. Can you please _____? I am trying to concentrate here," said Daisy to her screaming brothers.

   (A) shut up
   (B) get up
   (C) wake up
   (D) pull up

9. If I am going to _____ for this, I am taking you down with me," said the thief to the drug lord.

   (A) sit down
   (B) cut down
   (C) go down
   (D) run down

10. When she got back from her studies in Munich, Rosemary had _____ a classy dresser with a taste only for the branded.

   (A) turned on
   (B) turned through
   (C) turned up
   (D) turned into

281. OPEN SOMEONE'S EYES

Meaning:
To cause someone to notice or be aware of something important

Example:
The experience really opened his eyes and changed the way he felt about his life.

Now make your sentences.
1. _____.
2. _____.
3. _____.

282. IN A PIG'S EYE.

Meaning:
This phrase is used to express strong disagreement meaning Never.

Example:
You want me to apologize to him? In a pig's eye!

Now make your sentences.
1. _____.
2. _____.
3. _____.

283. GET A MINUTE.

Meaning:
To have a quick break from responsibilities.

Example:
When I get a minute, I'll call for directions.

Now make your sentences.
1. _____.
2. _____.
3. _____.

284. GET AWAY.

Meaning:
To escape from something or someone.

Example:
Do you think you could get away for a couple of hours?

Now make your sentences.
1. _____.
2. _____.
3. _____.

285. CHANCES ARE...

Meaning:
This phrase means the likelihood of possibility of something to take place.

Now make your sentences.
1. _____.
2. _____.
3. _____.

TREASURE BOX:19

Read subjects that interest you in English. Start with simple books even children's books. Trust me! If you study well and right, you will speak and connect if you find yourself in the situation that you have to speak.

286. I CAN'T STAND...

Meaning:
We can use this in situations where we talk about things that we really dislike or hate:

Example:
I can't stand seeing animals suffer.

Now make your sentences.
1. _____.
2. _____.
3. _____.

287. TAKE EACH DAY AS IT COMES.

Meaning:
To deal with things as they happen, and not make plans or worry too much about the future.

Example:
There is nothing we can do we'll just take each day as it comes.

Now make your sentences.
1. _____.
2. _____.
3. _____.

288. LIVE UP TO.

Meaning:
To live in accordance with (expectations or an ideal or standard) or measure up to.

Example:
He never lived up to his father's vision of him.

Now make your sentences.
1. _____.
2. _____.
3. _____.

289. TOP PRIORITY

Meaning:
Something that is more important than other things.

Example: Make this task your top priority.

Now make your sentences.
1. _____.
2. _____.
3. _____.

290. GO TO/TAKE EXTREME MEASURES.

Meaning: To take a desperate action.

Example:
I have to take extreme measures to earn money by working on three jobs.

Now make your sentences.
1. _____.
2. _____.
3. _____.

Fill in the gaps with the best options.

1. "I can't __B____ the feeling that I am being watched," said the actress to her friends.

   (A) shake at
   (B) shake off
   (C) shake down
   (D) shake away

2. The car ____D___ the poor puppy and then sped off quickly.

   (A) ran off
   (B) ran past
   (C) ran into
   (D) ran over

3. The guard __C____ and let the nurse into the patient's room, not knowing it was the assassin in disguise.

   (A) stood over
   (B) stood back
   (C) stood aside
   (D) stood under

4. The story was ____B___ the eighteenth century and was about two lovebirds who were separated by their feuding families.

   (A) set down
   (B) set around
   (C) set off
   (D) set on

5. "I'm tired of people ___D___ on us. I want to make something out of myself," said Jack's oldest son, who is thinking of quitting school to go work.

   (A) looking for
   (B) looking between
   (C) looking after
   (D) looking down

6. Elle's fiancé ___C___ with her money and passport, and left her stranded at the resort.

   (A) got off
   (B) drop off
   (C) took off
   (D) cut off

7. "Something ___A___. I have to go. Let's do this another time," said Linda before running out of the diner.

   (A) came up
   (B) came over
   (C) came off
   (D) came around

8. Can you please ___A___? I am trying to concentrate here," said Daisy to her screaming brothers.

   (A) shut up
   (B) get up
   (C) wake up
   (D) pull up

9. "If I am going to ___C___ for this, I am taking you down with me," said the thief to the drug lord.

   (A) sit down
   (B) cut down
   (C) go down
   (D) run down

10. When she got back from her studies in Munich, Rosemary had ___D___ a classy dresser with a taste only for the branded.

(A) turned on
(B) turned through
(C) turned up
(D) turned into

291. CASH IN

Meaning:
1. Cash in something is to obtain money for something that you own

Example: She cashed in her stocks.
2. Cash in on something is to take advantage of something in order to make money.

Example: Carpenters cashed in on the construction boom.

Now make your sentences.
1. _____.
2. _____.
3. _____.

292. CLOCK UP.

Meaning:
Clock up something means to gain or reach a particular number or amount.

Example:
The basketball star clocked up a record number of baskets this year.

Now make your sentences.
1. _____.
2. _____.
3. _____.

293. AROUND THE CLOCK / ROUND THE CLOCK

Meaning:
This phrase means throughout the entire day and night: every hour of the day

Example:
Reporters worked around the clock to cover the story.

Now make your sentences.

1. _____.
2. _____.
3. _____.

294. BEAT THE CLOCK

Meaning:
This phrase means to do or finish something quickly before a particular time.

Example:
In a desperate attempt to beat the clock, I raced to mail my tax return before midnight.

Now make your sentences.

1. _____.
2. _____.
3. _____.

295. CARDINAL RULE.

Meaning:
This phrase means abasicprinciple or fundamental law

Example:
My cardinal rule is to always be honest.

Now make your sentences.

1. _____.
2. _____.
3. _____.

296. BE TAKEN IN

Meaning:

To be tricked or deceived by someone

Example:

He was taken in by a man who said he was collecting money for a charity.

Now make your sentences.

1. _____.
2. _____.
3. _____.

297. TAKE SOMEONE IN.

Meaning:

To offer someone food and shelter.

Example:

They agreed to take him in for the summer.

Now make your sentences.

1. _____.
2. _____.
3. _____.

298. BREAD AND BUTTER.

Meaning:

Abasic source of livelihood.

Example:

The automobile industry is the bread and butter of many Detroiters.

Now make your sentences.

1. _____.
2. _____.
3. _____.

299. TAKE SOMEONE`S LIVE.

Meaning:

To end someone's life.

Example:

The plane crash took the lives of all the people on board.

Now make your sentences.

1. _____.
2. _____.
3. _____.

300. A BRIGHTER FUTURE:

Meaning:

When something appears positive than before.

Example:

The doctor painted a brighter picture of the woman`s chances of surviving the cancer.

Now make your sentences.

1. _____.
2. _____.
3. _____.

Fill in the gaps with the following words.

**better, Into, Off, Over, Up, ahead, In,
along, lost, Out**

1. She doesn't speak English well, but she has been spending more time studying to get _____.

2. His friend told him that if he didn't listen to the teacher he would get _____ trouble.

3. We forgot to stop at the first station so now we have to get _____ at the second one.

4. She was so sick that she was taken to the hospital, but I hope she will get _____ her illness soon.

5. Let's get _____! It's late and we don't have any time to waste.

6. We can't get _____ until dinner because there is a traffic jam.

7. They're old friends and they've got _____ for a long time.

8. The police obliged the thief to get _____ of the car.

9. I plan to get some training so that I can get _____ in my career.

10. They're late. I suppose they got _____ because they didn't take the map.

301. TAKE ACTION

Meaning:
To do something.

Example:
Travelers want the airlines to take action to make flying safer and more comfortable

Now make your sentences.
1. _____.
2. _____.
3. _____.

302. TAKE IT FROM ME.

Meaning:
To believe something that someone tells you.

Example:
Take it from me. He would love to go to the concert with you.

Now make your sentences.
1. _____.
2. _____.
3. _____.

303. APART FROM.

Meanings and examples:
1) Apart from=not including
   I can meet you any day next week apart from Friday.
2) Apart from=in addition to
   He is multitalented, apart from singing, he also acts and paints.
3) Apart from= separated from
   It was the longest time we spent apart from each other.
Also, Apart from= Besides.

Now make your sentences.

1. _____.
2. _____.
3. _____.

304. "IN SPITE OF".

Examples:
1. In spite of the terrible weather, we had a really enjoyable day.
2. She decided to give up her job for his family, in spite of the high pay and fun.

In spite of = Despite (but without of)
1. She went to Greece for her holidays despite that she hates hot weather.
2. They visit the museum several times a year, despite having seen everything in it.
3. Despite the fact that the weather was terrible, we had a really enjoyable day

Now make your sentences.

1. _____.
2. _____.
3. _____.

305. SUPPOSED TO.

Case 1
Supposed to= generally believed.

Examples:
1. He is supposed to be rich.
2. This stuff is supposed to kill flies.
   Case 2

Supposed to =
a. What people are expected to do.
b. What is intended.

Examples

1. You're supposed to start work at 8:30 in the morning.
2. She was supposed to be here an hour ago. Where is she?
3. You're not supposed to park on the side of the road.
4. That is a strange picture. What is it supposed to be?

Now make your sentences.

1. _____.
2. _____.
3. _____.

306. CRACK SOMEONE UP

Meaning:
Make someone laugh very hard.

Example:
He really makes me crack up with his sense of humor.

Now make your sentences.

1. _____.
2. _____.
3. _____.

307. CRACK DOWN

Meaning:
To act more forcefully to regulate, repress, or restrain.

Example:
The police cracked down on speeding.

Now make your sentences.

1. _____.
2. _____.
3. _____.

308. PUT ONE'S LIFE ON THE LINE.

Meaning:

To risk death in order to try to achieve something.

Example:

Why would a man with a wife and three children put his life on the line for a stranger?

Now make your sentences.

1. _____.
2. _____.
3. _____.

309. MILE A MINUTE

Meaning:

very fast.

Example:

She talks a mile a minute and is very hard to keep up with.

Now make your sentences.

1. _____.
2. _____.
3. _____.

310. TWO SIDES OF THE SAME COIN

Meaning:

Different but closely related features of one idea.

Example:

Rewards and punishments are two sides of the same coin. Both are used to control people, and neither works very well.

Now make your sentences.

1. _____.

2. _____.

3. _____.

Fill in the gaps with the following words.

**lost, better, into, off, over, up, ahead, in,
along, out**

1. She doesn't speak English well, but she has been spending more time studying to get ____better_____.

2. His friend told him that if he didn't listen to the teacher he would get _____into____ trouble.

3. We forgot to stop at the first station so now we have to get _____off_____ at the second one.

4. She was so sick that she was taken to the hospital, but I hope she will get _____over_____ her illness soon.

5. Let's get _____up_____! It's late and we don't have any time to waste.

6. We can't get _____in_____ until dinner because there is a traffic jam.

7. They're old friends and they've got _____along_____ for a long time.

8. The police obliged the thief to get _____out_____ of the car.

9. I plan to get some training so that I can get _____ahead_____ in my career.

10. They're late. I suppose they got _____lost_____ because they didn't take the map.

311. THE OTHER SIDE OF THE COIN

Meaning:
A different and usually opposite idea about a situation

Example:
Being a parent is such a huge responsibility, but the other side of the coin is that it is one of the most exciting and enjoyable things you can do in life.

Now make your sentences.
1. _____.
2. _____.
3. _____.

312. LOSE STEAM.

Meaning:
To lose strength or inspiration.

Example:
The fundraising effort has lost steam.

Now make your sentences.
1. _____.
2. _____.
3. _____.

313. RIPPLE EFFECT

Meaning:
A spreading effect or series of consequences caused by a single action or event.

Example:
The oil policy tends to have a ripple effect throughout the economy as a whole.

Now make your sentences.

1. _____.
2. _____.
3. _____.

314. TAKE THE WORDS RIGHT OUT OF ONE'S MOUTH

Meaning:
To say exactly what someone meant to say before they have the chance to say it.

Example:
When you mentioned her dislike of fish you took the words right out of my mouth.

Now make your sentences.

1. _____.
2. _____.
3. _____.

315. THAT'S FOR SURE.

Meaning:
Absolutely correct.

Example:
They don't want any of us there this weekend, that's for sure.

Now make your sentences.

1. _____.
2. _____.
3. _____.

316. I'M GETTING........

Example:
A. "How are you enjoying your vacation?"
B. "I'm having a great time. How about you?"
A. "It's pretty fun here.
B. Ths. is a great place. I'mgettingcoldthough"
A. "Are you here with your family?"
B. "I'm here with my wife and 2 kids. They are so excited, here they come"
A. "Nice talking to you........

Meaning:
This phrase means you are about to obtain something.

Now make your sentences.
1. _____.
2. _____.
3. _____.

317. HAVE SOMETHING UP ONE'S SLEEVE.

Meaning:
To have a surprise or a secret plan or solution to a problem.

Example:
I've got something up my sleeve, and it should solve all your problems. I'll tell you what it is after I'm elected.

Now make your sentences.
1. _____.
2. _____.
3. _____.

318. YOU HAVE GOT TO BE KIDDING / YOU MUST BE KIDDING

Meaning:

I am very surprised and cannot believe you are serious.

Example:

You want me to drive into the city in this rain? You've got to be kidding.

Now make your sentences.

1. _____.
2. _____.
3. _____.

319. COME DOWN WITH SOMETHING

Meaning:

To become or to be sick with some illness.

Example:

Susan came down with a bad cold and had to cancel her trip.

Now make your sentences.

1. _____.
2. _____.
3. _____.

320. ON THE MEND

Meaning:

Recovering one's health.

Example:

I heard you had the flu, but I'm glad to see you're on the mend.

Now make your sentences.

1.   _____.
2.   _____.
3.   _____.

REVIEW: 16

Fill in the gaps with the following words.
get on, call off, turn down, switch on
look for, give up, put on, set up, brought up, make out

1. Due to lack of interest, we had to _____ the meeting.

2. The boy was _____ by a nanny.

3. The music is too loud. Could you _____ the volume, please?

4. It's dark inside. Can you _____ the light, please?

5. I don't know where my book is. I have to _____ it.

6. If you don't _____ the train now, it will leave without you.

7. Don't _____ singing. You are very talented.

8. Please _____ your coat, it is cold outside.

9. Would you like to _____ business in the United States?

10. I cannot _____ his writing.

321. PUT IT MILDLY

Meaning:
To say something without exaggeration.

Example:
It's a fairly long walk, to put it mildly-twenty miles or so.

Now make your sentences.

1. _____.
2. _____.
3. _____.

322. WHATEVER TURNS YOU ON/ WHATEVER FLOATS YOUR BOAT

Meaning:
Whatever excites you or interests you.

Examples:
a   I can't stand that kind of music, but whatever turns you on.
b. Ketchup on hot dogs! Yuck! But whatever floats your boat.

Now make your sentences.

1. _____.
2. _____.
3. _____.

323. I'M OUT OF HERE/ I'M OUTA HERE.

Meaning:
I am leaving this minute.

Example:
In three minutes I'm outa here.

Now make your sentences.

1. _____.
2. _____.
3. _____.

324. DROP EVERYTHING.

Meaning:
To suddenly stop what you were doing

Example:
Drop everything and go outside. The house is on fire!

Now make your sentences.
1. _____.
2. _____.
3. _____.

325. BY THE WAY.

Meaning:
A phrase indicating that the speaker is adding information.

Example:
Tom: Is this one any good?
Clerk: This is the largest and, by the way, the most expensive one we have in stock.

Now make your sentences.
1. _____.
2. _____.
3. _____.

326. ON THE ONE HAND

Meaning:
The first thing to consider is

Example:
On the one hand, I'd like more money, but I don't want to work extra hours.

Now make your sentences.

1. _____.
2. _____.
3. _____.

327. JUST IN CASE

Meaning:
Only if something happens.

Example:
i.   We keep a lot of food on hand, just in case there's a storm.
ii. Make sure you have extra batteries available, just in case.

Now make your sentences.

1. _____.
2. _____.
3. _____.

328. AS LONG AS

1.   For the period of time that.

Example:
You may keep the book as long as you want,

2.   Since, because.

Example:
Please pick up some milk as long as you are going to the store.

3.   Provided that.

Example:
As long as you don't expect it by tomorrow, I'll make the drawing.

Now make your sentences.

1. _____.
2. _____.
3. _____.

329. DYING FOR/DYING TO DO SOMETHING

Meaning:
Very eager to do something.

Examples:
i.   After a long hot day like this, I'm just dying for a cool drink.
ii. I'm dying to lock up and go home.

Now make your sentences.

1. _____.
2. _____.
3. _____.

330. THROW ONESELF INTO SOMETHING

1.   To jump into something, such as a body of water.

Example:
He stood on the bridge and threw himself into the river because he was unhappy with life.

2.   To dress in something hurriedly.

Example:
She threw herself into the dress. He just threw himself into his tux and ran on stage.

3.   To enter into or join something eagerly and wholeheartedly.

Example:

She threw herself into the project and helped immensely.

Now make your sentences.

1. _____.
2. _____.
3. _____.

REVIEW: 16. ANSWER

Fill in the gaps with the following words.
get on, call off, turn down, switch on
look for, give up, put on, set up, brought up, make out

1. Due to lack of interest, we had to __call_off__ the meeting.

2. The boy was ____brought up____ by a nanny.

3. The music is too loud. Could you __turn down____ the volume, please?

4. It's dark inside. Can you ____switch on__ the light, please?

5. I don't know where my book is. I have to __look for__ it.

6. If you don't ____get on__ the train now, it will leave without you.

7. Don't ____give up__ singing. You are very talented.

8. Please ____put on____ your coat, it is cold outside.

9. Would you like to _____set up____ business in the United States?

10. I cannot ____make out____ his writing.

331. HIGH AND LOW

Meaning:
Everywhere.

Example:
We searched high and low but couldn't find the ring.

Now make your sentences.

1. _____.
2. _____.
3. _____.

332. HAVE SOMEONE GOING.

Meaning:

To have someone believe something temporarily

Example:

You had me going for a minute there when you said my wife had been looking for me.

Now make your sentences.

1. _____.
2. _____.
3. _____.

333. TOUCH UP

Meaning:

To improve something by making minor corrections, changes, or additions.

Example:

The author touched an old essay up and submitted it for publication.

Now make your sentences.

1. _____.
2. _____.
3. _____.

334. FULL OF....

Meaning:
If something is full of things or people, it contains a very large number of them.

Example:
i.   They had a large garden full of pear and apple trees.
ii. His office was full of people.

Now make your sentences.
1. _____.
2. _____.
3. _____.

335. DOWN IN THE DUMPS

Meaning:
Unhappy.

Example:
She's down in the dumps because all her friends are married and out of town.

Now make your sentences.
1. _____.
2. _____.
3. _____.

336. THAT'S TOO BAD.

Meaning:
I'm sorry to hear that, unfortunate.

Example:
if you don't like it, (that's) too bad!

Now make your sentences.

1. _____.
2. _____.
3. _____.

337. ALL THUMBS

Meaning:
Very awkward and clumsy, especially with one's hands.

Example:
Mary is all thumbs when it comes to gardening.

Now make your sentences.

1. _____.
2. _____.
3. _____.

338. GEAR UP

Meaning:
To get ready or cause to get ready for coming action or event.

Example:
A group of investors had geared up for the takeover fight.

Now make your sentences.

1. _____.
2. _____.
3. _____.

339. GEAR TOWARDS

Meaning:
Organize or arrange something for a particular purpose, audience etc.

Example:

The project is geared towards older people.

Now make your sentences.

1. _____.
2. _____.
3. _____.

340. MOVE ALONG

Meaning:

To keep moving, not staying in one place.

Example:

The police told the crowd to move along.

Now make your sentences.

1. _____.
2. _____.
3. _____.

REVIEW: 17

Match the phrases with the meanings.

1. **Step Up.**   .to give money to (someone) for illegal or dishonest help.

2. **Buy off.**   .filling in for someone or doing well at an important thing.

3. **Have second thoughts.**   .to come or appear when not expected.

4. **Appeal to.**   .payment of something for another person.

5. *Come a long way.*   .to want something or someone very much.

6. **Advise against.**   .to be responsible for something.

7. *Treat.*   .to plead or make an earnest request.

8. *Answer for.*   .to recommend not doing something.

9. **Crop up.**   .to change your opinion about something.

10. **Ache for.**   .to make a lot of progress and improvement.

341. TAKE ONE'S EYES OFF SOMETHING OR SOMEONE

Meaning:
To stop looking at something or someone.

Example:
I couldn't take my eyes off of the waiter.

Now make your sentences.

1. _____.
2. _____.
3. _____.

342. FOR THE TAKING

Meaning:
Easily available.

Example:
If you're interested in the job, it's there for the taking.

Now make your sentences.

1. _____.
2. _____.
3. _____.

343. BOSS AROUND.

Meaning:
To tell others what to do.

Example:
Stop bossing me around. I'm not your employee.

Now make your sentences.

1. _____.
2. _____.
3. _____.

344. WHEN ONE IS GOOD AND READY.

Meaning:
when one is completely ready and willing.

Example:

I'll be there when I'm good and ready.

Now make your sentences.

1. _____.
2. _____.
3. _____.

345. WHEN ALL IS SAID AND DONE

Meaning:

when everything is finished and settled or when everything is considered.

Example:

When all is said and done, I believe I had a very enjoyable time on my vacation.

Now make your sentences.

1. _____.
2. _____.
3. _____.

346. TIME AFTER TIME / TIME AND (TIME) AGAIN

Meaning:

Repeatedly or over and over (again).

Example:

You've made the same error time after time! Please try to be more careful!

Now make your sentences.

1. _____.
2. _____.
3. _____.

347. WHERE HAVE YOU BEEN ALL MY LIFE?

Meaning:

An expression of admiration usually said to a lover.

Example:

John grasped Mary's hand, stared directly at her, andstuttered, "Where have you been all my life?"

Now make your sentences.

1. _____.
2. _____.
3. _____.

348. WHERE'S THE BEEF?

Meaning:

Something that you say when you think someone does not have enough ideas to make their plans work.

Example:

That's really clever and appealing, but where's the beef?

Now make your sentences.

1. _____.
2. _____.
3. _____.

349. WHEN THE TIME IS RIPE

Meaning:

At exactly the right time.

Example:

I'll tell her the good news when the time is ripe.

Now make your sentences.

1. _____.
2. _____.
3. _____.

350. HOW DID SOMETHING GO?

Meaning:
How successful was something?

Example:
How did your interview go?

Now make your sentences.

1. _____.
2. _____.
3. _____.

TREASURE BOX:20

Make your own vocabulary lists and review them often. Write sentences to help you remember what they mean just as in the other book. Use these new words and phrases in conversations and writings whenever you have the chance.

351. TONS OF

Meaning:
A very large amount or number of something.

Example:
We got tons of fried chicken, so help yourself.

Now make your sentences.

1. _____.
2. _____.
3. _____.

352. A SLIP OF THE TONGUE

Meaning:

A mistake you make when speaking, such as using the wrong word.

Example:

Did I say she was forty? I meant fourteen - just a slip of the tongue.

Now make your sentences.

1. _____.
2. _____.
3. _____.

353. TONGUE IN CHEEK.

Meaning:

If you say something tongue in cheek, what you have said is a joke, although it might seem to be serious.

Example:

My comment was made TIC. Don't take me seriously.

Now make your sentences.

1. _____.
2. _____.
3. _____.

354. GIVE SOMEBODY THE ROUGH SIDE OF YOUR TONGUE.

Meaning:
To speak angrily to someone.

Example:
The boss gave me the rough side of her tongue for being late twice this week.

Now make your sentences.
1. _____.
2. _____.
3. _____.

355. ON THE TIP OF ONE'S TONGUE

Meaning:
Ready to utter something but unable to remember it at the moment.

Example:
I met him last year and his name is on the tip of my tongue-it'll come to me in a minute.

Now make your sentences.
1. _____.
2. _____.
3. _____.

356. ON THE WRONG SIDE OF SOMEONE.

Meaning:
To be out of favor with someone.

Example:
I do what I can not to get on the wrong side of people.

Now make your sentences.

1. _____.
2. _____.
3. _____.

357. GET UP ON THE WRONG SIDE OF BED.

Meaning:
Be in a grouchy, irritable state.

Example:
What's got into Max today? Did he get up on the wrong side of bed?

Now make your sentences.

1. _____.
2. _____.
3. _____.

358. ON THE WRONG SIDE OF THE LAW

Meaning:
In a situation in which you are doing something illegal

Example:
Being on the wrong side of the law is not unusual for many people in this part of town, be careful of who you hang out with.

Now make your sentences.

1. _____.
2. _____.
3. _____.

359. I HATE TO SAY/ADMIT OR I HATE TO TELL YOU.

Meaning:
It is used for showing that you are sorry about what you are going to say, because you think it is unpleasant or you wish it was not true

Example:
i.   I hate to say this, but I think you've probably lost your money.
ii. I hate to say it, but I was glad when he went home.

Now make your sentences.
1. _____.
2. _____.
3. _____.

360. ZIP AROUND.

Meaning:
If you zip around, you move quickly from place to place.

Examples:
1.   Miho was in a hurry so she zipped around the supermarket, tossing all the things she needed into her trolley as she went.
2.   Steve is our courier and he spends all day zipping around town on his bike, picking up and dropping off packages and documents.
     Try to make your own sentence so you will remember.

Now make your sentences.
1. _____.
2. _____.
3. _____.

REVIEW: 18

Are these sentences true or false? Check.

		True	False

1. To *bear fruit* is to produce a desired result or reward.

2. Skin someone alive is hurt someone with a tool.

3. Settle for is to accept something that is not quite satisfactory.

4. To devote to something is to give a lot of your time or money to it.

5. Take the plunge is to give up on doing something.

6. Over-the-top means that you fall off of a boat.

7. Flavor of the month is someone or something that is temporarily popular.

361. WIND UP

Meaning s and examples:

1. To Finish or put an end to something.
   Before ***winding up*** his speech he thanked everyone for their presence.

2. To finally arrive in a place.
   We wound up in a village with a fantastic view.

Now make your sentences.
1. _____.
2. _____.
3. _____.

362. WRAP UP.

Meanings and examples;
1. To cover or to enclose
   She's busy wrapping up her Christmas presents.
2. To complete a task or a discussion.
   The salesman hoped to wrap up a few deals.

Now make your sentences.
1. _____.
2. _____.
3. _____.

363. ZONE OUT

Meaning:
If someone zones out, they look blankly ahead without paying attention, maybe because they're tired, bored or affected by drugs or medication.

Examples:
1. Ricky sometimes zones out when he's bored in class. He looks like he's a million miles away.
2. I was talking to Debbie, but she was so zoned out that she didn't even hear me.

Now make your sentences.
1. _____.
2. _____.
3. _____.

364. HOPE FOR THE BEST

Meaning:
To desire the best to happen.

Example:

Good luck on your interview. You know we all hope for the best.

Now make your sentences.

1. _____.
2. _____.
3. _____.

365. CALL IT A DAY

Meaning:

Stop a particular activity for the rest of the day.

Example:

It's past five o'clock so let's call it a day.
Similarly, call it a night means "to stop something for the rest of the night,"

Now make your sentences.

1. _____.
2. _____.
3. _____.

REVIEW: 19

Fill in the gaps with the right phrasal verbs.

1. Can you _____ _____ with some solutions.

2. If we don't start spending less, we will ___ ___ of money soon.

3. I'm going to ___ ___ down on fatty foods.

4. He likes to _____ _____ up stories.

5. I ___ ___ well with Sandy because she is so easygoing.

6. I don't want to cook. Let's _____ _____ out.

7. Let's ___ _____ up the tent before it rains.

8. It's warm. Why don't you _____ _____ off your jacket?

9. Don't _____ _____ to me you rude boy.

10. The bomb will _____ up in two minutes.

11. I need to get _____ of some old furniture.

12. _____ up! It's morning.

REVIEW: 20

Match the highlighted phrasal verbs with the best definition on the right:

(a) The gas heater **blew up** and destroyed the house.	do again
(b) Can you **take care of** my dog while I'm away?	choose
(c) If you **come across** a post office, can you buy some stamps?	get up
(d) Did anybody **come up with** a solution?	look after
(e) This year I'm going to **cut down on** junk food.	quit
(f) There are so many mistakes we'll have to **do** it **over.**	exploded
(g) I **dropped by** friend's house on my way home.	arrived
(h) His grades were so bad that he decided to **drop out of** university.	met by chance
(i) Do you want to order in or **eat out**?	used up
(j) I don't **get along with** Jack so I'd prefer if you didn't invite him.	stand, bare
(k) Why don't you **look up** his address in the phone book?	delay
(l) You can't trust him because he **makes up** stories all the time.	think of
(m) She **picked out** a long black dress to wear.	Find by chance
(n) We **put off** our vacation plans until next year.	reduce
(o) I am not going to **put up with** the noise and garbage anymore.	eat at a restaurant
(p) I want to **get rid of** some old clothes.	Have a good relationship
(q) I **ran into** my old friend at the movie theater.	visit
(r) Our car **ran out of** gas so we had to walk two hours to the gas station.	undress

(s) After we **set up** the tent, we started to make dinner.	answer rudely
(t) He **showed up** two hours late.	make quieter
(u) You should **take off** those wet clothes.	arrange
(v) Jake **talked back to** his mother so his mother punished him.	tell lies
(w) I **turned down** the volume after the neighbors complained.	search for, find
(x) I usually **wake up** at five in the morning.	remove, throw away

Congratulations for making it to the end! You deserve a treat!

Remember to go back and complete the exercises that you have left behind. Try as much as possible to remember all the tips in the **treasure boxes**. Also remember that practice makes perfection. You need to apply what you have learned by **cooking** your English and by speaking to native speakers and by surrounding yourself with English, in other words, by living it, to be able to produce the desired result which is, to **connect**!

Happy learning!